W9-AXH-054

FERNAND LÉGER
A PAINTER IN THE CITY

SERGE FAUCHEREAU

FERNAND LÉGER
A PAINTER IN THE CITY

EDICIONES POLÍGRAFA, S.A.

© *1994 Ediciones Polígrafa, S. A.*

Balmes, 54 - 08007 BARCELONA (Spain)

Reproduction rights © V.E.G.A.P., Barcelona, 1994
Text copyright © Serge Fauchereau
Translated by David Macey
Designed by Jordi Herrero

I.S.B.N.: 84–343–0748–0
Dep. Leg.: B. 5.919 - 1994 (Printed in Spain)

Colour separations by
Teknocrom, S. A., L'Hospitalet de Llobregat (Barcelona)
Printed and bound by La Polígrafa, S. L.
Parets del Vallès (Barcelona)

CONTENTS

Autoportrait (Self-portrait). 1930. Pencil, 12 ⅝ × 9 ¼ in. (32 × 23.5 cm).
Musée National Fernand Léger, Biot. Gift of Nadia Léger and Georges Bauquier.

FERNAND LÉGER
A PAINTER IN THE CITY

No matter which period of his career they date from, surviving photographs and descriptions of Fernand Léger show an affable, simple man wearing a checked cap. His moustache gives him a rugged but kindly look. Many people have been deceived by the image of a peasant who is fascinated by the city. 'He has a suburban mind', said his friend Blaise Cendrars. The simplicity of the man seems to be at odds with the range and power of both his visual works and his thinking. We fall for the illusion only because we fail to look at his paintings carefully, to think about their conspicuously immediate effect, and to pay attention to his writings. Léger produced an impressive body of writing over a period of more than forty years. Some artists, like Braque and Picasso, are visual ascetics who work pragmatically and in silence, but others, like Malevich and Mondrian, base their asceticism on a process of theoretical reflection which has to be taken into account if we are to understand anything of their approach to aesthetics. In intellectual terms, Léger has more than a little in common with Malevich, despite their many artistic differences. It is no accident that relations between Mondrian and Léger were always cordial, nor that Malevich devoted some very insightful pages to Léger's work.

An enormous amount has been written about Léger's work, but at risk of stating the obvious, I admit that I have not consulted all the brilliant, serious or repetitive studies that have been devoted to him over the last half century and more. Given the narrow compass of the present study, there would in fact be little point in doing so. Léger's visual *oeuvre* raises a large number of problems and, rather than attempting a frustrating overview, it seems preferable to concentrate on some of the most basic questions, and to identify the key ideas that underpin it in its entirety. The best way to do so is to turn to contemporary accountsm —from Apollinaire, Le Corbusier and a few others — and above all to the painter's own writings. It is not in fact difficult to reach the conclusion that Léger's own comments, which should be referred to as often as possible, provide the liveliest and most significant introduction to his work.

An Artist's Career

Fernand Léger was unaffected by the turmoil that surrounded the existence of a Vincent van Gogh or the highly publicized private and public life of a Picasso. He was neither a *peintre maudit* nor a painter who lived in the limelight, and it might be said of him, as it can be said of Ingres or Cézanne, that, despite his fairly extroverted character, his paintings, his public activities and his published writings tell the whole story. This does not mean that he did not have a private live like anyone else or that he was untouched by marriage, divorce or other disruptive incidents. He kept all that secret, and it never became part of his work. His unique paintings are impersonal and are quite non-anecdotal. The intrusions into the private lives of creative artists that are so highly prized these days will teach us nothing about them. Although it remained uneventful, his career is nonetheless a good example of tenacity, intelligence and integrity.

Léger was born in Argentan (Orne) in 1881, and nothing and no one destined him for an artistic career, least of all his family, for whom 'learning a good trade' was the only thing that counted. 'If my father had lived a few years longer, I would have become a cattle dealer like him. No doubt about it. I was a strapping lad, I loved physical strength, and I loved to watch the oxen in the fields. The life of a big stockbreeder is amazing — and I would certainly have been drawn to the physical side of its strong, sturdy roots' (*L'Intérieur de l'art*, interview with Dora Vallier, Paris: Le Seuil, 1982, p. 52). As he showed a talent for drawing, he was sent to study architecture in Caen (1897–99) and was later employed by an architect in Paris. After his military service, he was finally drawn to painting. He studied at both the École des Arts Décoratifs and at the Académie Julian, as well as at the Beaux-Arts — but unofficially, as he failed the entrance examination. He supported himself by working as an architectural draughtsman and a photographic retoucher, and by doing odd jobs. He painted in the impressionist style, but kept very few of the paintings done in the years between 1905 and 1907. His encounter with Cézanne's painting, on the other hand, marked a turning point for him, and he moved into La Ruche, a former wine warehouse which was home to a colourful community of artists and bohemians ranging from Archipenko to Soutine, from Chagall to Lipchitz.

In 1909, Léger painted a few cubist paintings, including *Le Compotier sur la table*. Was he encouraged to do so by the example of Braque and Picasso? He was close to Guillaume Apollinaire and especially Robert Delaunay, who become his friend, and had made the acquaintance of Douanier Rousseau. But it was the poet Blaise Cendrars who was to become his alter ego from 1911 onwards. Cendrars's aesthetic and attitude was so similar to Léger's that, on reading their respective writings, one wonders more than once if it was the poet who influenced the painter or vice versa. It was in fact a case of a perfect meeting of minds. It was, however, not until 1911 that Léger made his mark by exhibiting a startlingly original canvas at the Salon des Indépendants. It was *Nus dans la forêt*. Léger was thirty. That Picasso already had a whole *oeuvre* behind him at the same age is an indication of how slow Léger had been to mature. He had now made a name for himself. He exhibited and gave lectures, and Apollinaire hailed him as one of the major cubist painters.

The war that broke out in 1914 marked a turning point, for both better and worse. Léger was immediately mobilized and sent to the front. The positive side to the war was that it allowed him to discover for the first time the comradeship of ordinary people, while the sight of the machines was a brutal challenge to his conception of aesthetics. Less positively, Léger was gassed on the Verdun front in 1916. He was invalided out of the army, returned to civilian life and went back to painting. When peace was restored, Apollinaire and Duchamp-Villon were both dead; Braque and Cendrars had been lucky to survive. A new age was beginning, and art had to face up to the future. Paintings like *Les Disques* (1918), *La Ville* (1919), *Le Mécanicien* (1920) and *Le Grand Déjeuner* (1921) were an embodiment of the new spirit. Léger was therefore one of the first artists Le Corbusier and Amédée Ozenfant turned to when they founded their journal *L'Esprit Nouveau* (1920–1925). Léger was now active in a number of different areas. He illustrated books (Cendrars, Goll), and developed what was to be a lasting interest in ballet and the cinema. He enjoyed major successes with the Ballets Suédois: *Skating Rink* in 1922, and *La Création du Monde* in 1923. In the cinema, he collaborated with Abel Gance and then Marcel L'Herbier, before making his own *Ballet mécanique* in 1924. That same year, he founded the Académie de l'Art Moderne with Ozenfant. Although he was to teach for many years, teaching never interfered with his artistic activities, and nor did it prevent him from travelling widely. He took an interest in architecture, attempted to make painting an integral part of it and executed various mural compositions, whilst at the same time continuing to practice a starkly purist easel-painting: *Le Balustre* (1925), *L'Accordéon* (1926). Le Corbusier and Mallet-Stevens asked him to decorate their respective pavilions at the 1925 Exposition des Arts Décoratifs.

By the end of the 1920s Léger was beginning to look in a new way at objects — flowers, stones, garments or locks — and to depict them either outside any context, or in unexpected combinations. The famous *Joconde aux clés* of 1930 is one example. *Les Trois musiciens* of 1930 and *Marie l'acrobate* (1934) are, however, proof that he still retained his affection for the plastic form of the human body. Although Léger continued to work in the studio, to teach and to travel throughout the 1930s, the period was, above all, marked by major public and private commissions. Taking part in international exhibitions in Brussels in 1935 and in Paris in 1937 gave him a much wider audience. This was one of Léger's great concerns, as he made clear during the *Querelle du réalisme* debates in 1936. As a result, he attempted to bring modern art to a working-class audience by exhibiting in factories and popular cultural centres.

The outbreak of war in 1939 put a sudden end to this period. Being *persona non grata* in the eyes of the German occupation forces and their collaborators, Léger had to flee to the United States in the autumn of 1940. He made a living as best he could among the other exiled artists, surviving with the help of American friends and by lecturing and teaching in various universities. New themes began to appear in his paintings: the series of divers, acrobats and cyclists.

Between his return to France in December 1945 and his death in 1955, Léger seems to have been at the height of his creative career. This was the period of large-scale masterpieces like *Les Loisirs* (1948–1949), *Les Constructeurs* (1950), *La Partie de campagne*, *La Grande Parade* (1954). Léger now extended his range of activities. As well as producing a wide variety of two-dimensional works — easel-paintings, etchings, stage designs — he began to take an interest in sculpture (*La Grande Fleur polychrome*, 1952). Public commissions finally allowed him to establish the dialogue with architecture that had always interested him. He created a huge mural panel for the United Nations Building, mosaics for a church in Assy and for Gaz de France in Alfortville, and stained glass windows for a church in Audincourt and for the University of Caracas. When he died, the world discovered to its stupefaction that the man who had quietly practiced his painterly craft with such calm passion was a universal figure and that his death left a major gap in the art of our century. He was, said Pierre Reverdy in a final farewell, 'a man who was able to hold his own against the times in which he lived, and all that implies, who could adapt to the surging rhythms of time'.

From Impressionism to Cubism

Fernand Léger preserved almost none of his juvenilia. The earliest surviving paintings date from 1905. *Portrait de l'oncle de l'artiste* (fig. 2) is simply the work of a conscientious student. It is one of those classical and commonplace portraits that he would later judge so harshly: 'When you have spent six months at the École des Beaux-Arts, you know how to do a portrait: all the École pupils know how to do a portrait of their grandmother. That doesn't prove that they have any talent' (*Functions of Painting*, Tr. Alexandra Anderson, London: Thames and Hudson, 1973, p. 144). *Le Jardin de ma mère*, which dates from the same period, is much more interesting because the artist is deliberately working within the tradition of the impressionists. Léger always celebrated impressionism as the first movement to have freed form and colour from the obligation to imitate, to which painting had previously been confined. 'The impressionist revolution was dazzling; it destroyed chiaroscuro, did away with lines around volumes, abandoned local colour and, after a heroic battle, imposed pure colour, and construction as opposed to complementary colours' (unpublished text, cited Roger Garaudy, *Pour un réalisme du XXᵉ siècle*, Paris: Grasset, 1968). This is a good description of *Le Jardin de ma mère*, where the subject is delineated by touches of pure colour. Yet while it is easy, with hindsight, to see in it all the characteristics of the Léger of the future — bright colours, contrasting round and rectangular forms — there was nothing particularly original about the painting in 1905. Léger quickly moved on, and began to learn from Cézanne. Dissatisfied with the flickering effect produced by some impressionist paintings, the painter from Aix had begun to redefine form and drawing — as had Gauguin and the Nabis, though their suppression of depth and their technique of outlining flat drawings threatened to reduce painting to decoration. The more austere Cézanne turned, rather, to geometry and reorganized the space of the canvas as he began to paint nature in terms of 'the cylinder, the sphere and the cone', as his celebrated formula put it. In the various landscapes he executed during his stays in Corsica, Léger tentatively moved in the same direction; his drawing became more pronounced, and his colours more restrained.

After moving into the Ruche in 1908, Léger met many artists and writers. He was not unacquainted with the analytic cubism of Picasso and Braque. *Le Compotier sur la table* (1909, fig. 5) is very similar to their work. The artist rearticulates his space and forms in terms of a series of planes that suggest depth — the fourth dimension of painting, acording to the theorists of the day — and the overall effect is monochromatic. This was no more than an experimental phase. Sophisticated research into tonality that involved lingering over the details of a still life or concentration on the same old guitars, pipes and fruitbowls was alien to Léger's temperament. He was too much of an extrovert to work like Picasso and Braque, and had no interest in metaphysical speculations. An introspective exploration of the substance of painting had so little appeal for Léger that, unlike the genuine cubists, he never showed any interest in *papiers collés* and collage (the very late and rare exceptions to the rule are playful rather than anything else). His first truly personal painting (*Nus dans la forêt*, 1909–1910, fig. 6) is a literal application of Cézanne's principles. It is a large-scale canvas on which he worked for a long time. Its first viewers could only make out a roughly hewn geometric mass, and

La Couseuse (Woman Sewing). 1910. Oil on canvas, 28 ³/₈ × 21 ¹/₄ in. (72 × 54 cm). Musée National d'Art Moderne, Centre Georges Pompidou, Paris. Gift of Louise and Michel Leiris.

talked of 'tubism'; those who thought it natural to find fauns and nymphs in a forest sniggered at the idea of nude woodcutters. The astute and more poetic Guillaume Apollinaire remarked in his *Peintres cubistes* that: 'The woodcutters' bodies bore the scars their axes had left on the trees and the overall colour had something of the greenish, underwater light that filters down through the foliage.' Perhaps because of his muscles and rhythmic movements, it is in fact more architypical than it might seem to liken a woodcutter to a mechanical form. Look at the painting and then read these words. 'One of the big trees had been chopped through, and standing beside it, with an uplifted axe in his hands, was a man made entirely of tin. His head and arms and legs were jointed upon his body, but he stood perfectly motionless, as though he could not stir at all.' The reader may have recognized the Tin Woodman in Frank Baum's *The Wizard of Oz* (1899), though the painter and the writer were obviously quite unknown to one another. Throughout this period, Léger's figures retain this mechanical look. *La Couseuse* of 1910 (p. 9) is an assemblage of jointed tubes; rather than being, as has been claimed, descended from the Douanier Rousseau, Léger's woman seems, even more so than the woodcutters, to have stepped out of a 1950s science-fiction film; she also has an astonishing resemblance to the Tin Woodman in Victor Fleming's film (1939) — but she does not derive from

Cézanne. It is possible that there is an element of mischief in the multiple cylinders, spheres and cones of the large *Étude pour trois portraits* (fig. 9): the woman flanked by the two children does look somewhat caricatural. Even at the time, Apollinaire, who had already noticed Léger, expressed something of this uncertainty in his review of the Salon des Indépendants in the spring of 1911: 'His art is difficult. He is creating, if I can put it this way, a cylindrical painting, and does not always avoid giving his compositions the unplanned look of a pile of tyres. No matter! His self-imposed discipline will put some order into his ideas, and the originality of his talent and his palette is already noticeable.'

Léger did not spend long on this exaggerated Cézannism and by 1911 was already moving towards a more relaxed cubism. Brief as it may have been, it should not, however, be forgotten that his 'tubist' period anticipates the calmly geomtrical figures that he would paint a few years later.

Léger and Delaunay were close friends. They were not satisfied with what they saw around them. They were attracted to neither the fauves nor Matisse, whom they admired from afar. Fauve lyricism seemed to them to be the logical successor to impressionism. In comparison, the extreme freedom of their old friend Rousseau seemed to them to be the result of a real discipline, even if he was a *naïf*. Nor were they greatly interested in the more resolutely revolutionary Braque and Picasso. Léger often told an anecdote that captures their differences. The two friends went to the Galerie Kahnweiler, he told Dora Vallier, 'And we saw, along with old Delaunay, what the cubists were doing. Surprised by their grey canvases, Delaunay exclaimed: "*But these lads are painting with spiders' webs!*"' The world of the cubists was inward looking; the calm of the studio allows greater concentration. Léger and Delaunay preferred the bustle of the streets. Picasso and Braque's favourite subjects were lonely musicians or, better still, still lifes; and they painted them with such perfection that only Gris could, in his own way, go any further in that direction. Léger, like Delaunay, was restless; he wanted both more colour and more dynamism, and it is well known that the two go together. In 1910-1911, he executed a large painting which completely overturned his earlier conceptions: *La Noce* (fig. 8). *Nus dans la forêt* and even *Étude pour trois portraits* still used perspective to give form to the geometricized elements and to produce an effect of general depth. While *La Noce* and the other paintings executed in 1911-1912 still employ perspective, it is now a multiple perspective which disperses the subject and breaks it up with quite non-representational planes. The non-representational planes surround and penetrate the recognisable elements. In *La Noce* and *Les Fumeurs* (1911, fig. 7) those elements are still indicated by shading; in the *Femme en bleu* of 1912 (fig. 13), they become flatly geometrical areas of pure colour. Colour, bright, strong colour, has returned; and the problem of colour was to be one of Léger's lasting preoccupations. From now on, colour explodes as multiple perspectives disperse the elements of the subject into an explosion of colour; figures and landscapes, which had until had been kept distinct, are dispersed in accordance with the requirements of the painting and not the subject: the painting — a spatially defined object — takes control of the work of the painter. The canvas is no longer a sort of window on to an element of reality, but an isolated object like a chair, a stove or any other object in the studio. Are the wedding guests in *La Noce* sitting at a table? Or are they in the street — we can see rows of trees and houses among the figures? The question is not really relevant: this is a painting, and whether it was a real or an imaginary marriage is relatively unimportant.

Movement — rapid in the case of *La Noce* and slow in that of *Les Fumeurs* — is scarcely less important than colour. How to express movement was, of course, a question which tormented many artists at a time when new technologies (cars and planes in particular) were changing perceptions of landscape. F.T. Marinetti's futurist manifesto of 1909 had deified speed as absolute beauty ('A roaring motor car, which seems to run on shrapnel, is more beautiful than the Victory of Samothrace') and a small number of Italian artists — Boccioni, Balla Carrá, Severini — were working along the same lines. It was not until 1912 that they revealed their work to the public, and there is therefore no possibility of their having influenced Léger. We simply have to accept that the question was in the air. The sentimental arguments the Italian futurists used to support their theories were quite alien to Léger. His dynamic is above all visual: it is addressed to the eye, and has no literary overtones. It is certainly based upon colour, but form is still more important. For Léger, form was a search for visual dynamism and not, as it was for the futurists, a way of capturing speed. The puffs of smoke and the series of trees in *Les Fumeurs* are not an expression of time, and could not be further removed from the futurists' flurries. Léger is working within a plastic realm whose dynamics are based on a effect which is easily described, if not easily employed: the contrast between rectilinear and curved forms. Referring to the paintings of this period, which often feature smokers and smoke, Léger stated in 1914 that 'Here you have the best example on which to apply research into multiplicative intensities. Concentrate your curves with the greatest possible intensity without breaking up their mass; frame them by means of the hard, dry relationship of the surfaces of the houses, dead surfaces that will acquire movement by being coloured in contrast to the central mass and being opposed by live forms; you will achieve a maximum effect' (*Functions of Painting*, p. 16). The dynamism created by the contrasting curves and straights is all the greater in that the painting represents a move away from figuration and towards a well-considered layout which does not actually allude to the real world. *Fumées sur les toits* (p. 11) and *Passage à niveau* (fig. 12) are far removed from *Femme en bleu* (fig. 13), though all were painted in 1912. In the former, everything is still identifiable — the houses, roofs, windows and trees — but it takes a certain concentration to

Fumées sur les toits (Smoke on the Rooftops). 1911. Oil on canvas, 21⁵⁄₈ × 18¹⁄₂ in. (55 × 47 cm). Staatliche Kunsthalle, Karlsruhe.

perceive a hand or a glass in *Femme en bleu*. What is more, we are now quite definitely in a purely visual realm that is far removed from the Italian futurists' search for atmospherics or feelings. This does not mean that Léger was unaware of how modern technology and speed affect the way we perceive the world; on the contrary, he was probably indirectly influenced by futurist theories when he declared in 1914 that: 'When one crosses a landscape by automobile or express train, it becomes fragmented; it loses in descriptive value but gains in synthetic value. The view through the door of the railroad car or the automobile windshield, in combination with the speed, has altered the habitual look of things. A modern man registers a hundred times more sensory impressions than an eighteenth-century artist' (*Functions of Painting*, p. 11). Léger is definitely a modern artist.

The object on the canvas now consists of nothing more than somewhat recognizable fragments. The three dimensions have become confused and colours no longer correspond to any naturalism. The external subject is no longer even a useful pretext. In 1913, Léger developed a theory of contrasts that led him to pure abstraction. *Contraste de formes* (fig. 17) piles up truncated polychromatic cones against a ground of blue and white stripes. This abstract Cézannism disturbs the viewer all the more in that the painter seems to feel no need to match a colour with its complementary or to give any depth to the painting as a whole: the truncated cones float in a two-dimensional space.

At this point in his evolution, was Léger about to join the Kandinskys and the Kupkas, who came to abstraction by very different routes? Léger always took an interest in his abstract colleagues, and respected them — Mondrian in particular. But his feet were too firmly on the ground, and he was too happy to be involved in a dialogue with the modern world that surrounded him, to opt for true abstraction. Few of Léger's paintings make no reference to the real. *Le Réveille-matin* (fig. 19), which is so similar to *Contraste de formes*, reconstructs a world. The metal cylinder of an everyday object radiates (or perhaps rings) throughout the whole space of the picture, turning the figure in the armchair and its surroundings into a vast field of contrasted forms. This was painted in 1914 and the forms of the real world refuse to leave the painting. Léger will never abandon them. *Femme en rouge et vert* (fig. 20) is a step in that direction, and *Village dans la forêt* a further step. The masterpiece of the period is, perhaps, *Escalier* (fig. 16). Metallically modelled 'robots' go up and down flights of angular steps. This is an anonymous and animated crowd on an escalator in a department store or a station, and not the single nude descending a staircase painted by Léger's friend Duchamp. It was in fact at this point, notes Duchamp, that Léger began to experiment with the palette of primary colours that would later dominate all his paintings: red figures, blue figures and yellow staircases. At the same time, drawing comes back into its own: the coloured forms are clearly delineated and outlined in black. From now onwards to *La Joconde aux clès* of 1930 and until the final canvases (*Les Constructeurs* of 1950 or *La Grande Parade* of 1954), it is not difficult to see the extent to which Léger's work is governed by the law of contrasts.

War broke out. Mobilized on 2 August 1914, Léger suddenly had to break off his beloved work. As he explained to the Swedish painter Nils Dardel in 1915: 'I was trying to do some fairly abstract research (contrasts between forms and colours) in a large painting that was to have been called *L'Escalier*. The war took me and prevented me from achieving what I wanted to achieve. If I am lucky enough to be able to continue my work, I will go back to it with energy and pleasure' (*Léger och Norden*, Stockholm: Moderna Museet, 1992). Throughout his life, Léger often liked to say that the war had been a major turning point for him. He spoke of his discovery of the great fraternity of ordinary men, and of his astonishment at seeing 'the open breech of a 75 mm gun in the bright sunlight'. It is clear that this made a lasting impression on the man. The anecdote about the breech of the 75 mm gun has been taken literally by Léger's commentators, and not least by his friends Cendrars and Ozenfant. The latter wrote: 'Fernard Léger was impressed by the formidable machine of modern warfare and specific objects like guns, shells and weapons ... Of all the known artists of the pre-war period, he is probably the one who has changed most' (*Art*: Paris: Budry, 1928). It was a long time before another painter, Jean Bazaine, felt bold enough to contradict this cliché: 'It seems to me quite futile to see the war as the decisive element that led Léger to what is

Dessin du front (The Front). 1916. Pencil, 7 ¹/₂ × 6 ¹/₄ in. (19 × 16 cm).
Musée National Fernand Léger, Biot. Gift of Nadia Léger and Georges Bauquier.

La Cuisine roulante (Field Kitchen). 1916. Ink, 7 ³/₄ × 6 in. (19.7 × 15.4 cm).
Musée National d'Art Moderne, Centre Georges Pompidou, Paris.

conventionally but somewhat clumsily called a "mechanized vision". There was as much mud in the war as there was steel. And the whole of Léger's *oeuvre* is potentially there in the headstrong and tumultuous canvases he was painting before 1914' (*Le Temps de la peinture*, Paris: Aubier, 1990). This should be blindingly obvious to anyone who is prepared to look carefully at *Nus dans la forêt*, *Femme en rouge et vert*, at the drawings and watercolours executed by Léger at the front, and then at the *Soldat à la pipe* of 1916 and *La Partie de cartes* of 1917 (figs. 22 and 23). They all derive from his "tubism", and *La Partie des cartes* is scarely more disjointed or more metallic than *Nus dans la forêt*. In his *Partie des cartes*, Léger is merely systematizing the principles Cézanne had revealed in the *Joueurs de cartes* he painted in the late 1890s, and was well aware of the fact. His letter to Dardel goes on: 'The war was too late in taking me to have had any influence on me. I will continue my efforts, with the same tendencies'. When he had completed his painting, Léger reworked certain elements of it so as to 'explore' them still further. The result was *Etude pour la Partie de cartes*, dated 1918 (fig. 31).

In 1929, Malevich published a fine commentary on paintings like these in the journal *Nova Generatsia*: 'He now paints nothing but screws and motors, and human beings themselves are treated as though they were iron or machinery: his human beings have lost their flesh, their blood and their souls, and Léger replaces them with his own feelings, his own soul; as a result, the motors, screws and human beings are dissolved into a new order created by the artist's temperament.' They are indeed machines, but the human and emotional element is still there in certain signs, if we look closely enough. In *La Partie de cartes*, for example, Léger carefully emphasizes the fraternity which, regardless of rank, underlies the scence by very precisely differentiating the three soliders he depicts: the man in the helmet appears to be a private from a line regiment; we can tell that the man taking the trick is a staff sergeant because he is wearing stripes and *Médaille militaire*; the third man appears to be an officer wearing the *Légion d'honneur* or the *Croix de guerre*. After his return to civilian life, Léger did not paint any more scenes from the front, but for some time he did go on making use of anecdotal details. *Le Cirque* (1918, fig. 26) depicts a theme to which Léger would return at regular intervals throughout his life; minor representational details are scattered across the canvas, like a wink in the middle of a complex geometrical pattern: a performing dog sits up and begs in front of the man swinging on the trapeze; a white clown jumps up and waves between two polyhedrons. Fernand Léger is all too rarely given credit for his sense of humour.

Between *La Partie de cartes* and these circus paintings, something changes. It is noticeable that the rounded, modelled elements are projected forwards, especially in *Acrobates* (fig. 27), whereas the background tends to be organized into a single plane. The same effect can be seen in other works from 1918: *Le Remorqueur rose* and *Les Hélices* (fig. 24 and 25). The background is flat, and the flatness is emphasized still further by the fragmentary inscriptions, which seem to have been stencilled — a technique which Braque had already used before the war to remind the viewer that a painting is merely a two-dimensional surface. The change is gradual. Léger was a thoughtful artist and the changes in his work result from a slow process of maturation; this is why there are often several studies or variants on the same subject. Although some of the characteristic themes (machines, spectacles) have something in common with futurism, they have none of futurism's freneticism. Léger was certainly enthusiastic about the modern world, but he was not intoxicated by speed. He liked the calm strength of tug boats rather than the thrust of the racing cars that were so dear to the futurists or the soaring aeroplanes that fascinated his friend Delaunay. Typically, he always captures his acrobats and sportsmen in moments of equilibrium or suspended motion. In that sense, he was still close to the cubists. Léger's *Les Hélices* is a dynamic painting because the elements are segmented into colour-planes, but everything about it is static, whereas Delaunay's *Hélice* (1923), which deals with the same subject, depicts a whirling movement and the virtual shape produced by the revolving propeller.

Léger's continued reflections on depth and visual dynamism were taking him back to abstraction. The contrasted forms now had less to do with the expression of volume than with the form and colour of the flat areas. Allusions to anything real are rare in *Le Disque* (fig. 33), and completely absent from *Les Disques* (fig. 30), which is the masterpiece of 1918. The canvas is ostentatiously flat, and marked by the violent contrast between the angular shapes and the disks. Delaunay's disks shimmer with light, and are distantly derived from neo-impressionism; Léger's disks are hard and precise, and look like the wheels and gears of a machine, and they are in fact connected by rods and joints. We are in a colourful industrial world which is full of movement. Solitary meditations in cubist studios are a thing of the past.

Architecturalizing Painting: Today

Les Disques marked the beginning of a new phase. It was the result of Léger's visual research rather than of some revelation vouchsafed by a gun-breech during the war or by the advertisements in the Place Clichy. In his own view, another large-scale and slightly later work dating from 1919 represented a major accomplishment: *La Ville* (fig. 29). Léger explained why he liked it so much on several occasions, notably in an interview with Dora Vallier: 'I used flat surfaces because a plane surface is a faster construction. Modelling slows down the eye. This certainly derives from a loathing of academic modelling and I studied flat areas more and more when I began to take an interest in murals .... Flatness has an instantaneous impact, and it is perfect for large-scale murals. The great battle between flat tones and modelling in my painting had begun: I wanted to achieve a more direct form, and modelling is much less direct than flatness. Afterwards, when I had solved the question, I began to use modelling again, but I used it freely, only when I wanted to slow down the form and not where it was needed to give the impression of volume.' This *a posteriori* analysis was obviously made in the light of all his later evolution, but it does reveal the themes the painter would develop from now onwards: a complex interplay between flatness and modelling, between abstract and representational elements that is far removed from any naturalism. Unlike *Disques*, *La Ville* is not entirely flat. The central section reworks the theme of a staircase and robotic-looking figures; the remainder is flat but not systematically non-representational, as we can recognize silhouettes, letters and metallic structures. The uncertainty as to the painting's spatial location is very stimulating for both the eye and the imagination.

It probably took Léger some time to formulate his own principles clearly and to master them completely. *Le Typographe* (1919), *La Femme au miroir* and *Les Trois Camarades* (1920, figs. 28, 39 and 37) are, perhaps, still too derivative of the cubist aesthetic. *L'Homme à la pipe* (1920, fig. 38) combines, in a spiral movement set against orthogonal planes, an abstract setting, and a man and dog handled with a surprising and almost naive stylisation. *Le Mécanicien* (1926, fig. 40) and the 'tugs' series (1920-1923, figs. 34, 35 and 54), on the other hand, are masterpieces of balance.

Le Mécanicien suggests that the Douanier Rousseau's straightforward and charming representationalism had swept away cubism (look at the similarity between it and the *Portrait dit de Pierre Loti*, which is also set against a background of smoking factories). It is true that cubism had had its day. The war had dealt it a heavy blow and Picasso, its main pioneer, had for some years been making sorties into openly representational art. In 1918, Amédée Ozenfant and Edouard Jeanneret (Le Courbusier) published their book *Après le cubisme*, which outlined a new order: purism. They were primarily theorists whose practice was serious to the point of being arid but, even though he was not influenced by it at the time, their definition of a painting as 'a device for moving people' had something in common with the reforms Léger was introducing. As Cendrars put it in 1919, Léger was rebelling against the 'spiders' webs' of pre-war cubism:

'Some cubist canvases weave such an unexpected, disturbing and unhealthy spell that they remind one of black-magic rituals... That is why the youth of today — healthy, muscular and full of life — is turning away from them' (*Aujourd'hui*, Paris: Grasset, 1931, p. 110). The last sentence provides an excellent description of *Le Mécanicien* and of the hopes of a new post-war generation which wanted to enter the new era on a new footing. Cendrars also made a prophecy: 'I therefore foresee lots of colour, new colour.' For contemporary observers, it was quite obvious that Léger was the main architect of a renaissance. André Salmon, for instance, wrote in 1920: 'Now that form's salvation was ensured, Fernand Léger was the first to want a rebirth of colour, and he was definitely one of the most successful artists to pursue that path. Wasn't that because he was a natural colourist and because there is such a thing as talent, whatever anyone may say?' (*L'Art vivant*, Paris: Crès, 1920, p. 131). Salmon's comments are a good description of how Léger was striving for a return to drawing and colour, both of which had been reduced to a mimimum in the pre-war cubism of Picasso and Braque. Léger set colour free by using it light-heartedly. He used pure tones and avoided complementary colours, but, unlike any naturalist he also applied colour evenly: in Léger, human silhouettes can be green or red, cows can be orange and tree trunks can be blue. His forms — both representational and abstract — stand out all the more clearly because they are picked out by outlining or very simple modelling. Before long, the painter would divorce colour and drawing completely. But everything was done in moderation because 'Too much colour, no colour' (*Functions of Painting*, p. 82).

Léger liked to tell a very revealing anecdote about the impact mechanization had on artists at the beginning of the century. 'Before the 1914 War', he told Dora Vallier, 'I went to see the Salon de l'Aviation with Marcel Duchamp and Brancusi. Marcel, who was a sardonic man and difficult to pin down, wandered around amongst the engines and propellers without saying a word. Then he suddenly spoke to Brancusi: "Painting's finished. Who could improve on that propeller? Could you do that?" He was very attracted to such precise things. So were we, but not in such an absolute way. Personally, I was more drawn to the engines and the metal than the wooden propellers.' We know that Duchamp quickly abandoned easel-painting, and began to give an artistic status to *ready-mades* like bicycle wheels and bottle racks. Brancusi, in contrast, turned away from industrial objects and began to create very pure forms which were sometimes biomorphic, or abstractions derived from the natural forms of animals or human beings. Of the three friends, only Léger took up the challenge of industrial objects, of the formal perfection of engines and the great coloured clamour of advertizing posters. This was such a crucial element in his aesthetic that we will have to come back to it many times. 'My era surrounds me with manufactured elements that are so perfect, so complete.

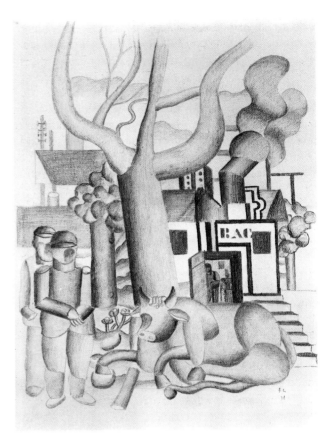

Paysage animé (Animated Landscape). 1921. Pencil, 16 ⅝ × 11 ¾ in. (42.1 × 29.9 cm). Rijksmuseum Kröller-Müller, Otterlo.

Paysage animé (Animated Landscape). 1921. Pencil, 14 × 10 in. (35.6 × 25.4 cm). Rijksmuseum Kröller-Müller, Otterlo.

I wanted to make something as beautiful — a magnificent aeroplane propeller, part of a machine, a beautiful stone picked up on a beach. I don't mean copying it, but making something as good' (previously unpublished manuscript, cited *Pour un Réalisme du XXe siècle*, p. 65). Léger never copied; he transformed industrial or natural objects as he saw fit (as we can see, he attaches equal importance to propellers and stones), fragmented them to meet the needs of his paintings, and indulged in all kinds of syntheses. In his view, a purely imaginary mechanical structure is worth as much as the most elaborate still life. Look at his *Eléments mécaniques* (figs. 55 and 57), which are anything but 'vanities'. 'The machines are there, with their beautiful optimism', said Blaise Cendrars.

Delaunay was one of the few French painters of the day to take an optimistic view of machines. The cubists had little or no interest in factories of their products. The fauves either distrusted and avoided them (Matisse) or, like Vlaminck, denounced 'Machine bogots': 'Factories: money for bread, rent, clothes, alcohol, cards and the cinema. Having sampled those pleasures, you go to bed unhappy or drunk... And you go back to your machine, because if you don't go back to it, you lose it all! You become more attached to it as its hold on you increases. At the same time, it is wearing you down morally with its monotonous hum and with the fastidiously repetitive gesture it forces you to make.' (*Le Ventre ouvert*, Paris: Corréa, 1937, p. 2). It is true that Léger's enthusiasm for every incarnation of modernity can be surprising. There is something naive about this shrewd man's enthusiasm for New York, where he saw only the lights and the technology and not the filth and the ghettoes, or for the Spartakiades. He was enchanted by the precision of the formation marching and forgot about the slogans and the indoctrination. This was probably not so much naivete on the part of the man as an overwhelming desire to grasp the positive side of things, a passionate quest on the part of an artist who was interested in everything that might enrich his art. As early as 1923, he himself answered the objection: 'I have certainly no intention of shouting from the rooftops that "That's all there is to it". The mechanical element, like everything else, is only a means, not an end' (*Functions of Painting*, p. 28).

Being a modern man, Léger wanted no aspect of the modern world to escape him; we will be coming back to this point several times. He therefore constantly clashed with those who claimed that the landscape had not changed since Corot, with those who thought figures should look like photographs or heroic and mythical chromos. As he stated on more than one occasion, his own masters were the pre-Renaissance artists who freely invented their subjects rather than copying them, or David and Ingres, whose desire for classicism allowed them to reconstruct landscapes and bodies as they saw fit.

Man and his environment had changed greatly over the previous century. What had been bucolic landscapes were now crisscrossed with roads and railways. They had sprouted factories, telegraph poles and electricity pylons, and were broken up by enormous advertizing billboards. No painter could ignore this: 'Now the railroads and the automobiles, with their plumes of smoke or dust, seize all the dynamic force for themselves, and the landscape becomes secondary and decorative. Posters on the walls, flashing advertizing signs — both are the same order of ideas' (*Functions of Painting*, p. 13). It is because it was the point where the metropolis met what remained of the village that Fernand Léger was so fond of suburbia. In his *Paysages animés* of 1921 (p. 14), he takes a

Étude pour La lecture (Study for 'Reading'). 1923. Pencil, 12 ⅝ × 9 ⅞ in. (32 × 25 cm). Musée d'Art Moderne, Villeneuve d'Ascq. Gift of Geneviève and Jean Masurel.

Étude pour La lecture (Study for 'Reading'). 1923. Black pencil on bistre paper, 10 ⅝ × 14 ⅝ in. (27 × 37 cm). Musée d'Art Moderne, Villeneuve-d'Ascq. Gift of Geneviève and Jean Masurel.

Étude pour Le grand déjeuner (Study for The Luncheon). 1921. Pencil, 19 ¼ × 14 ⅜ in. (48.8 × 36.5 cm). Rijksmuseum Kröller-Müller, Otterlo.

Étude pour Le grand déjeuner (Study for The Luncheon). 1921. Pencil, 14 ⅝ × 20 ¼ in. (37 × 51.4 cm). Rijksmuseum Kröller-Müller, Otterlo.

delight in showing that the angular factory with its tree-like and smoke-plumed chimneys is so close to the rural world of plants and animals. There are as many curves and straight lines, and as much colour, in one as in the other, and the painter therefore accords them the same value in his visual composition. The figures do not receive any special treatment; like the rest of the painting, they are an interplay of lines and coloured surfaces. Seen from a distance, they have the stiff, solid look and the uniform colour of the robots that were popularized by Wegener's *The Golem* (1920), and then by post-Second World War science fiction. When we look at them more closely, they are archetypes and not individuals. *Le Mécanicien* is a perfect example. The monochrome figure stands out against a background structure of girders painted in flat, bright colours and, even in repose, the muscular figure is a perfect evocation of the connecting rods, joints and moving parts of a powerful machine. The face reveals no attempt to capture any psychological expression. Everything about the painting is solidly constructed and unambiguous; the colours are sober and precise, and everything speaks of strength and serenity.

'For me', said Léger, 'the human body is no more important that keys or velocipeds. It's true. For me, these are plastically valuable objects to make use of as I choose' (*Functions of Painting*, p. 155). This is the painter speaking, and it does not mean that Citizen Léger attached no more importance to a man than to a stone or a bicycle. The confusion of the two — or the confusion of aesthtics with sociology or moralism — leads to misunderstandings and to the absurd theses of those who insist on seeing Léger as the poet of dehumanization: 'With a terrible sincerity, he is describing to us the man of the society of the future: a dehumanized being made by an engineer in the image of the

world through which he moves: a glacial, metallic world made of pistons, connecting rods and gears. This is no longer a drama involving man and machine; this is a mechnical man whose limbs and brain — which is quite devoid of love and understanding — are merely elements of the gigantic machine that surrounds him and controls him' (Bernard Champigneulle, *L'Inquiétude dans l'art aujourd'hui*, Paris: Mercure de France, 1939, p. 129). Such blindness in the face of art has never been rare; yet paintings should not be read as though they were documents, or through literary spectacles misted up with misplaced sentimentality. Like Léger's other paintings, *Le Mécanicien* is not an expression of individuality. Léger is not trying to portray an individual in his psychological or physionomical singularity, but to compose a painting representing a man, a modern man.

The human figure is central to a whole series of paintings executed between 1920 and 1925. Massive figures, most of them female, stand or recline in an interior. 'They have', writes Maurice Raynal 'a serenity and weight that reminds one of good statuary' (*Anthologie de la peinture en France*, Paris: Aubier, 1927, p. 210). Between *Les Deux Femmes et la nature morte* of 1920 (fig. 41) and *La Lecture* of 1924 (fig. 56), something definitely changes. The extent to which the bodies are disjointed varies. Facial features that were almost non-existent in 1920 gradually become clearer over the next few years, and eventually become quite definitely pronounced. That they are stereotypical, all the same and impassive makes them all the more impersonal, but does it have to be pointed out that that Léger was not interested in portraiture? These interchangeable faces are signs, just as a circle is a breast (and the figures usually have only one) and just as a wavy black line is a head of hair.

Discussing *Le Grand Déjeuner* (1921, fig. 44) with Alfred

J. Barr, Léger stressed his *classicism*: 'One background of classicism dominate in myself, I believvwe, some romantic pranks as: *La Ville* (1919), *Les Disques* (1920) or *Les Plongeurs* (1941–1942) but some women's bodies, one table, a dog, every time's subjects without any expression of evocation. It is the classical line, at my opinion [*sic*]. To put the subject or the object inside, behind the pictorial expression. The romantic is just the contrary, I believe; the subject or object come before, in expressive feeling. I have lived this uneasiness all my life and *Le Grand Déjeneur* is one of my classical fighting won [*sic*]' (*Léger's 'Le Grand déjeuner'*, Minneapolis Institute of Art, 1980, p. 72). The tradition Léger claims as his own obviously includes Ingres's

Le Bain turc and his odalisques, and Chassériau's bathers. Léger accentuates the curves and elongated limbs, and redistributes the body across the space of his painting. Ingres's *Grande Odalisque* (1814) was criticised for having three verterbrae too many, for having no elbows and for being too uniform in tone. Even in Ingres's day, copying was confused with creating — creating a harmonious body of forms and colours. In Léger, the subject is, as he puts it, so far 'behind' its pictorial expression that we can see a great similarity between compositions like *Deux Femmes et la nature morte* (figs. 34 and 41) and *Pont du remorqueur*, or between *Le Grand déjeuner* and his *Grand Remorqueur* (figs. 44 and 54).

Moving Image: Object-Spectacle

Léger's interest in the cinema — a new form of spectacle — probably dates from before the Great War. Apollinaire and his friends were passionately interested in the cinema, and the painter Léopold Survage had thought of making an abstract film, in colour, entitled *Le Rhythme coloré* ('Coloured Rhythm'). Léger must have known about it, as Survage described his plans in the July 1914 issue of Apollinaire's journal *Les Soirées de Paris*, which also reproduced several of Léger's paintings. The writers Blaise Cendrars and Riciotto Canudo, who were both close to Léger, devoted a lot of their time to the cinema. A statement from Pierre Reverdy in the journal *Nord-Sud* in October 1918 captures the fascination the cinema exerted over the whole of this generation: 'On seeing certain films, I have felt emotions that were *more powerful* and at least as pure as those I have felt on seeing my favourite works of art.'

Far from seeing the 'seventh art' (the expression is Canudo's) as a challenge to painting, Leger quickly realized that it offered painting more interesting possibilities than the simulacra and static transpositions of the futurist painters. In 1919, he illustrated a curious screenplay by Cendras entitled *La Fin de monde filmée par l'ange Notre-Dame* ('The End of the World filmed by the angel Our Lady'); they both hoped that it would be filmed. Abel Gance showed some interest in it, but finally employed Cendras as his assistant on another film: *La Roue* ('The Wheel'). The film was shot betwen 1919 and 1921, and had music by Arthur Honegger. Léger did not collaborate on it directly, but did act as a technical adviser when some scenes were shot (rails and points; a moving locomotive). Léger was enthusiastic about the film because, as he put it, 'the mechanical element plays a predominant role'. In other words, his enthusiasm had a lot to do with his own preoccupations. As for the plot, he seems to have little interest in it, even at this early stage; a plot was merely a pretext for beautiful images. A 'machine' theme is not,

however, sufficient justification for a film. *L'Autre Aile* ('The Other Wing'), which Canudo adapted from one of his own novels, dealt with aviation, but despite the multiple shots of fuselages and propellers, the film is still a mediocre sentimental story which is stagey rather than cinematic — significantly, Canudo used it as the basis for a lavishly illustrated 'visual novel' that is the ancestor of the photo-novel.

Because the plots are flimsy and because the physical action is more varied and more intense, Léger also preferred ballet to plays, which he found too stilted and too close to the day to day experience of the audience. In Léger's view, the world was a pretext for a vast spectacle, which would be all the more successful if it succeeded in disorienting the audience: popular festivals, circuses, music halls, churches, shops, and stalls in the street were all spectacles, but film was the spectacle that was most likely to draw an audience. It is

La **Création du monde: Étude de rideau** (The Creation of the World: Study for Curtain). 1924. Gouache, 16 1/8 × 22 1/2 in. (41 × 57 cm). Photo: Giraudon.

difficult to establish precisely when he resolved to make a film. In about 1921, he wrote the screenplay for a cartoon — *Charlot cubiste* ('A Cubist Chaplin'). He also made a painted wooden Charlie Chaplin, which was part mobile relief and part jointed puppet. Perhaps he was thinking of the jointed *Danseuse* Severini had made in 1916.

Charlot cubiste was never made. Ballet, however, is not too far removed from puppetry and animation. A group of Swedes with an interest in both dance and painting — Rolf de Maré, the dancer Jean Börlin and the painter Dardel — had recently founded the Ballets Suédois in Paris. They knew Léger and asked him to design the sets and costumes for a ballet based on a story-line by Canudo, with music by Honegger: *Skating Rink* (fig. 50). The setting and characters appealed to Legér's love of sporting spectacles, games and popular dance halls. The ballet was set in a skating rink where various characters come to enjoy themselves, and where they come into conflict. He designed the costumes in such a way as to divide the characters into two sub-divided groups: men and women 'of the people', and men and women 'from the world of fashion'. The sets, in contrast, were abstract and brightly coloured planes. Léger saw the dancers as 'mobile sets', as three-dimensional forms moving in front of flat coloured planes.

Skating Rink had its première in January 1922; the next ballet, *La Création du monde* (figs. 45–48) opened in October 1923. The latter was much more ambitious. Conceived by Cendras as a 'negro' ballet, it was quite in keeping with Léger's liking for African idols and masks. The two friends initially thought of asking Erik Satie to write the music, but Darius Milhaud, who at the time drew much of his inspiration from jazz, proved to be a judicious choice. 'Léger wanted to interpret primitive art and to paint the curtain and scenery with African deities which could express the power and the darkness' wrote Milhaud. 'He would have liked to use balloons representing flowers, trees and all kinds of animals. They were to have been filled with gas, and would have floated up at the moment of creation. The project came to nothing, as it would have meant having a complicated arrangement of gas bottles at each corner of the stage, and the noise of the balloons being inflated would have drowned out the music. Léger had to content himself with taking his inspiration from animal costumes based on those worn by African dancers during their religious ceremonies' (*Notes sans musique*, Paris: Julliard, 1949). The dancers now really were moving sets: their bodies were formally unrecognizable as they were clad — or even encased, as Léger wanted them to move stiffly and mechanically — in extraordinary costumes and disturbing masks. They crawled on the floor and walked on stilts. They were contrasted with the trees painted by Léger, which grew out of the stage, and with various moving planes. 'The point was', wrote Léger at the time, 'to make a break between the visual atmosphere of a room and that of the stage, to make the individual disappear in order to utilize human material, to create fiction on stage. The

human material appeared, but it had the same spectacle value as the object and the decor' (*Functions of Painting*, p. 38).

In 1923 the film-maker Marcel L'Herbier asked Léger to design sets for him, but the theme was now science fiction rather than barbarism. In order to make his spectacular *L'Inhumaine* ('The Inhuman Woman', fig. 49), L'Herbier brought together the best artists of the day. It was not the tragic and silly adventures of his rather unconvincing *femme fatale* that made his film a landmark, but Milhaud's music, Mallet-Stevens's sets, Pierre Chareau's scenery and, above all, Fernand Léger's designs. As the film's crucial scene takes place in a scientist's laboratory, Leger designed a vast set in the style of his machine paintings. Intelligently shot by L'Herbier, these sequences are hallucinatory. On the whole, however, the film is in the tradition of Louis Feuillade's adventure films — just as René Clair's contemporary *Entr'acte* is in the comic tradition of Méliès's films. In Léger's view, this was a dated style. Unfortunately, he was not familiar with the work Eggeling, Richter and Ruttmann were doing in Germany, but even their animated geometry did not really investigate the *object* in the way that he wanted to investigate it. Lèger later had the opportunity to work on another science fiction film with a much more satisfying screenplay by H. G. Wells. Alexander Korda, who produced the film, contacted Léger in 1934, but times had changed, and Léger's machine period had long been over. In a disenchanted letter, he wrote to Rolf de Maré: 'It's a strange life here. I'm doing the costumes for a film Wells is making with Korda. Much more difficult than one imagines. This is far from the freedom we had working on your ballets' (*Léger och Norden*, p. 91). In any event, Léger did not work on *Things to Come*.

It was probably after working on *La Création du monde* and *L'Inhumaine* that Léger embarked on the making of *Ballet mécanique*, in which objects really were manipulated by the dictates of his fantasy. We know from a letter written to René Clair at the beginning of 1923 that at this point Léger was still thinking of an animated film. But, with the help of a young American cameraman called Dudley Murphy, he in fact made a real film. Man Ray is said to have worked on it, and Léger gives Ezra Pound credit for some kaleidoscopic effects — Pound in fact used a technique previously developed by the photographer Alvin Langdon Coburn to create multiple images of his *vortographs*.

When his film was released (November 1924), Léger replied to a survey carried out by *Les Cahiers du mois* with a short profession of faith about painting and the cinema. 'The future of both the cinema and painting lies in their interest in objects, in fragments of objects or in purely fantastic and imaginative inventions. Painting's mistake is the subject. The cinema's mistake is the screenplay. The subject, literature, sentimentalism, or in other words having to compete with the theatre, are all negative values that clutter up today's cinema. Real cinema is *an image of an object we have never*

Le Ballet mécanique. 1924. Extract from film.

seen with our own eyes, and it can be very moving if it is presented properly.' At this point in the history of the cinema, which was still silent, all experimental film-makers were agreed that the new art's subordination to literature — meaning third-rate novels and plays — was something to be condemned. As early as 1921, a young protégé of Cendrars named Jean Epstein had declared in peremptory terms that 'The cinema is bad at telling anecdotes. And dynamic action in a film is a mistake' (*Cinéma, bonjour!*, Paris: La Sirène, 1921). The avant-garde of the day believed that this *pure* new art should be based upon the rhythm of images alone. In the same issue of *Les Cahier du mois*, René Clair, who had just shown *Entre'acte*, wrote: 'Thought is almost as fast as the fleeting images. But it slows down, is defeated and gets a surprise. It gives up. The screen is a new gaze, and it defeats our passive gaze. It is at this point that rhythm can be born.' In the same issue, Germaine Dulac added: 'The total film

we all dream of composing is a visual symphony made up of rhythmical images, coordinated and projected on to the screen by an artistic sensibility' (*Les Cahiers du mois*, Nos. 16–17, 1925, pp. 107, 13, 64). All these comments could be applied to *Ballet mécanique*, were it not that Léger, as we have seen, wanted something more plastic, something independent of any screenplay, whereas professional film-makers faced with commercial imperatives could only occasionally do without one. Clair in fact abandoned the avant-garde; Epstein and Dulac turned to documentaries and then gave up making films. The price Léger paid for his freedom was commercial failure; a few prints circulated (13 to 14 minutes; there is even a variant that was partly tinted by Léger) and were admired by professionals and amateurs alike, but the general public stayed away.

A disjointed puppet — Chaplin — appears on the screen and doffs his cap. A woman on a swing. Repeated smiles.

The swing, upside down. Balls and reflections. Geometric forms oscillate; multiple images seen through a prism. Eyes. A close-up of a collection of cake tins. The head of a round-eyed parrot, more mechanical than animal. Sets of prisms, bottles, straw hats moving to a jerky rhythm. Figures, swaying bowls and egg-whisks, a mechanical smile. A fairground. Soldiers and lorries. A piston and a connecting rod. Machines, machines. Egg-whisks, machines, pistons, connecting rods, a washerwoman. The film moves backwards and forwards as the washerwoman goes up and down a staircase. Title: 'Five-million dollar pearl necklace stolen.' String of pearls, a string of zeros. A mule-collar. The mule-collar in the shape of a smile. The rigid face of a woman. The clown-like head of a wooden model. Geometric shapes. Swaying cake-tins and lids. Pans in a display window. Geometric arrangements of artificial legs. Faces in mirrors. A series of bottles seen from different angles. Chaplin bows and breaks up as he cavorts about. A woman smells some flowers…

Even though the human element recurs throughout *Le Ballet mécanique*, it is the mass-produced industrial objects that hold one's attention. People who would have enjoyed watching a twirling ballerina or flowers were shocked by twirling objects — pans and egg-whisks — which are not normally accorded any poetic value, as though poetry were a matter of objects and not what one can do with objects. We now know that the aim was to make the audience look at mass-produced objects in a new way: Léger painted or filmed sieves, Duchamp exhibited a snow-shovel, while Satie used the sound of typewriters and Milhaud set the text of a catalogue of agricultural machinery to music. These were not inconsequential gestures. A few decades later, Arman would make piles of pincers and suitcases, Rancillac would paint magazine covers. Klasen would paint electricity meters, Cage would prepare pianos with nails, keys and bolts, and Kagel would use the sound of water being poured into a basin. They all had different intentions, but the object — that damned object — has won its artistic credentials.

There are obviously many more fleeting and insistent images in *Le Ballet mécanique* than can be described here: neither the eye nor the memory can retain them all. The fact that the film is so conspicuously placed under the aegis of Chaplin is a good indication that humour plays a large part in it. Germain Dulac said, for instance, that *Le Ballet mécanique* was *ironic*. Its ironic quality emerges much more clearly from the sound version, in which Antheil's score is played by a strange orchestra of player-pianos, sirens, propellers, with a large percussion section echoing the images of kitchen utensils and motors. The entire mechanical ballet is dominated by objects; their presence is more insistent and frequent on the screen than that of the living elements. Both are shot from the same angles. They are seen in series and in groups. They are shot in close-up, and details are isolated. We see multiple and fragmented objects as the film speeds up and slows down. Images are repeated, move, and are seen from different angles. The images are so unusual as to be frequently unrecognizable. The repeated close-up of the smiling lips seen in isolation from the face becomes a purely mechanical movement, and one is unsure whether it is a set of gears or the indentations of a pastry mold. The dancing boaters and bottles are more human than the upside-down figure on a swing; the close-up of the belly of a swaying salad-shaker handle is as mysterious as the kaleidoscopic shot of a parrot's head. What a visual adventure! In order 'to provide variety and contrast,' said Léger, he also inserted 'a few picturesque moments and *postcards*, which are meaningless in themselves; they relate and react to the images that come after them' (*Europe*, no. 508–509, August–September 1971, p. 64). These short scenes seem to have been taken from other films: the woman smelling flowers, or the roundabouts and automata from the Luna Park fairground remind one of the fairground sequences in Epstein's *Coeur fidèle* (1923). Other elements, again inserted for the sake of contrast, are more specifically pictorial: Léger's own paintings, or simple geometrical surfaces — decentred circles that prefigure Duchamp's *Anémic cinéma*; green, red, and then yellow and blue triangles in the coloured version in Rolf de Maré's collection in Sweden.

The way in which the rhythm of the ballet brings its elements together can be humorous, as when it makes an implicit analogy between the impassive face, with its austere make-up and severely painted lips, and the clownish wooden head from Luna Park, and as when a contrast is drawn between a submissive turn-of-the-century impressionist woman with her coiled hair, and a modern woman — an androgyne wearing bright make-up, with her short, straight hair slicked down. Other movements suggest an underlying leimotif: the movement of the pistons and connecting rods reappears in the mechanical movements of the washerwoman as she goes up and down the stairs, and in the repeated smile. The analogies and contrasts sometimes become extended metaphors, thanks to what Epstein called 'an aesthetic of succession and suggestion': 'Within the space of a few seconds, we have to grasp the meaning of ten metaphors, or we will fail to understand anything' (*La Poésie d'aujourd'hui: un nouvel art d'intelligence*, Paris: La Sirène, 1921, p. 174). And it is true that everything does happen very quickly. Immediately after the title 'Five-Million Pearl Necklace Stolen', we glimpse the string of pearls and then a string of zeros. Thanks to a contiguity of meaning, the lady's necklace will conjure up the mule's collar; read vertically and then horizontally, the oval of the necklace, of the collar, brings us back to the mouth and the movement of the lips. Epstein had described this a few years earlier: 'Projected on to the screen, I landed between the lips. What a vale of tears. Silent, too! Their double wings flutter and tremble, quiver, take flight, fly away and vanish: the splendid alert of a mouth opening' (*La Poésie d'aujourd'hui*, p. 171). So many suprises! And yet there is no story or plot, merely a play of motionless and moving shapes.

An Objective Art

Quite apart from its intrinsic qualities and its key position in the history of the cinema, *Le Ballet mécanique* was to have a direct influence on Léger's views on the visual arts. On the basis of these visual experiments, he would redefine the status of *objects* and of *realism* in his work. We have of course encountered both concepts before, but they were now to take on such importance as to dominate his thinking for many years to come. What interested him about the film camera was not so much the possibility of recording movement as the ability to see things differently, to enlarge them and fragment them, to see double or triple images of very different entities at the same time (for example, different-sized images of a woman's body or a salad shaker). Certain of his comments on *Le Ballet mécanique* could also be applied to his paintings: 'There are not only natural elements such as the sky, the trees and the human body; all around us are things man has created that are our new realism... used the close-up, which is the only cinematographic invention. Fragments of objects were also useful: by isolating a thing you give it a personality. All this work led me to consider the event of objectivity as a very new contemporary value... the thighs of fifty girls, rotating in disciplined formation shown as a close-up — that is beautiful and that is objectivity' (*Functions of Painting*, pp. 48, 50, 52). These important comments describe the various ways in which the objects of his new realism are situated.

Composition No. 1. 1927. Oil on canvas, 63 ³/₄ × 51 ¹/₄ in. (162 × 130 cm). Galerie Louise Leiris, Paris.

Natural and created objects: in Léger's *Nature morte* of 1927 (figs. 64 and 65), flowers and leaves are juxtaposed against a structure of planks, ball bearings and indeterminate objects, one of which is, curiously enough, decorated with a fish. In his *Composition* of 1929 (fig. 66), two milliner's models are juxtaposed against a leaf, a bunch of grapes and the tendrils of plants.

Close-ups: *L'Accordéon* (1926, fig. 60) depicts the instrument in profile, but we see only its essential elements; it takes up almost all the space in the painting, but it is completely flat and harmonizes with the background elements. *Roulement à billes* (1926, fig. 62), in contrast, retains the modelling and the blue glint of the steel; the bearing draws the eye all the more in that it is enlarged to an enormous extent and is the only recognizable element in the painting.

Fragments: in *Le Balustre* (1925, fig. 61) only one element, slightly larger than life, is retained of an entire staircase. In the *Guitare bleue et vase* of 1926 (fig. 59) only half of each of the objects depicted is visible.

Isolated objects: the flower in *La Rose* (1931, fig. 73) has no stem and no leaves, but takes up the entire space of the painting and its neutral grey ground. *Serrure* (1933, fig. 81) also depicts a single object. Even more so than the close-ups, this painting comes close to being abstract.

Multiple objects. Just as his film shows series of hats and bottles, some of Léger's paintings depict multiples of the same object: leaves in *Feuilles et coquillage* (1927 fig. 63), a line of three impersonal white profiles that underline the free composition of the rest of the painting in *Composition aux trois profils* (1937, p. 90).

In all these cases, the object — natural or man-made — is banal and utilitarian (keys, pipes, an arm, a musical instrument, a plant...) and must have a compositional purpose. Léger's compositional techniques vary considerably from one period to the next. Under the influence of the 'purism' of his friends Ozenfant and Le Corbusier in the years 1925–1927, Léger darkened his palette slightly to produce the austere verticals and horizontals of *Le Balustre*, *L'Accordéon* and *Nature morte aux feuilles mortes* (figs. 61, 62, 64). Over the next few years, the solidly constructed backgrounds tend to become emptier, and the even colour leaves the objects within the space of the painting itself. They no longer have any context. 'I felt that I could not put my object on a table without detracting from its value as an object', he explained (*L'Intérieur de l'art*, p. 71). At this point, the object, be it a mechanical or a vegetable element, usually stands alone, as in *La Rose* (fig. 73). But Léger very soon went back to compositions of objects that allowed contrasts. The most spectacular painting of this kind is the *Joconde aux clés* (fig. 68): the image of the famous figure painted by Leonardo da Vinci is associated with a large bunch of keys and a tin of sardines — a cultural object, an industrial object and a consumer object. It has nothing in common with either Duchamp's Dadaist gesture of painting a moustache on a reproduction of the *Mona Lisa* or with the surrealist image, which brings together two separate realities. Léger is interested in neither disconcerting short-circuits nor in iconoclastic provocation, but in visual contrasts. In order to demonstrate that, for him, the *Mona Lisa* was indeed an object like any other, he reworked the composition: the spatial positioning of the keys and the abstract forms remains the same, but the smiling woman is replaced by an umbrella. During the 1930s, Léger's researches into contrast became increasingly formal. The difference between the *Paysage* of 1931 (fig. 76), which is framed by two almost naturalistic trees, and the flat *Vase rouge et noir* of 1938 (fig. 89), in which no object can be identified, is a measure of the distance he had travelled. The forms and colours of vaguely representational compositions like *La Fleur polychrome* (1936, fig. 83) and *Le Grand coq bleu* (1937, fig. 92) prefigure the sculptures that the painter would execute in his final years.

As Léger's objects became so stylised as to be, if not abstract, at least unrecognizable in this period, the human body, which had until now been either disjointed or mechanized like a robot or a puppet, reasserts its presence, as though in reaction. *Contraste d'objets* (1930, fig. 71) returns to the familiar theme of the dancer. Her only role, however, is to provide a contrast with other forms: feathers or a bunch of keys. She could just as well be a little statuette, just as the Mona Lisa could well be a postcard. *La Danse* (1929, fig. 74) does, however, depict two actual characters. Their faces are expressionless, but their features are complete and their eyes have pupils. The flesh is more firmly modelled and the shoulders are visible. The frozen movement of the two dancers makes them appear to be floating against a background without any depth or any definite colour. The

only remaining free space in the painting is taken up by a long flower on a stem which underlines the movement of the dancers' bodies. The leaping motion of their *pas de deux* bends their arms and legs to make them form a rectangle inside the rectangle of the painting. The feeling that Léger's figures are floating gradually disappears in the following works. The female bodies in *Composition aux trois figures* (1932, fig. 79) are cropped by the bottom of the canvas, and seem to be more rooted in reality, even though the gate, the rope and the lichenoid shape – which may be a cloud – appear to be in state of levitation. The same elements reappear in many later paintings. *Marie l'Acrobate* (1934, fig. 88) seems to have her feet on the ground, as does — to some extent — the gate on which she has hung her clothes. Unlike the three nude graces in *Composition aux trois figures*, she is no longer a timeless figure, but a woman of our time. Her cropped hair emphasizes signs of femininity — the necklace, the loose costume — which had, until now, not usually been seen in Léger's figures. These paintings provided the basis for the very large scale works that would preoccupy Léger in the period 1935–1939. *Composition aux deux perroquets* (fig. 82) covers almost twenty square metres. It depicts three women and a man, but this is no Judgement of Paris, as at least one of the women is wearing a very contemporary cotton-print bathing-costume; the man's blue trousers, striped jersey, flannel belt and 'Sunday-best' pumps indicate that he is a worker on holiday — the costume has scarcely changed since the days when the impressionists went to paint on the banks of the Marne, and the parrots are no more suprising than the monkey on the leash in Seurat's *La Grande Jatte*. These figures enjoying a good time could well be circus people (they reappear in the drawing of *Acrobates et musiciens* of 1938, p. 22). Whoever they are, they certainly belong to our down-to-earth world, standing or sitting on the ground into which the gate posts are set. It would, however, be a mistake to believe that Léger's realism has

Acrobates et musiciens (Acrobats and Musicians). 1938. Black pencil on white paper, 19 ¼ × 25 ¼ in. (49 × 64 cm). Musée d'Art Moderne, Villeneuve-d'Ascq. Gift of Geneviève and Jean Masurel.

Les Grands Plongeurs noirs (Large Black Divers). 1944. Oil on canvas, 73 ⅝ × 86 ⅝ in. (187 × 220 cm). Galerie Maeght, Paris.

anything to do with verisimilitude. The curious little object by the gate and the carefully painted motifs on the uprights are included for plastic reasons: the two polychromatic little forms are a symmetrical counterpart to the two parrots. The other great composition of this period, which is entitled *Adam et Eve* (fig. 94) is similarly organized around the uprights of the bodies and posts, but the centre is no longer occupied by two figures. There are four movements to the rhythm of the painting. A large multicoloured bouquet occupies the centre and separates the two characters from the two uprights of the gate, where clothes and clouds are jumbled up together, but Léger himself said that 'elements like clouds, machines or trees have as much importance as figures.' Does the symbolism of the painting — and the even heavier symbolism of the title — mean that Léger was trying to go back to genre painting? Not at all, as the cloud and the clothes have the same solidly coloured presence as the couple. They are called Adam and Eve, but they might just as well be called Pierrot and Lisette. The man has a tatoo on his arm, and striped bathing costumes are not usually worn in paradise. As for the snake coiled around the stick, which may well have inspired the ironic title, it is probably part of the jugglers' act.

Léger had long been tempted to paint bodies intertwining to form a compact mass like a pile of objects. In 1925, he drew a group of three musicians (p. 30), and he reworked the drawing in 1930. In 1944, the same theme was reworked into a life-size composition in which the placement of the bodies remained unchanged. *Les Trois musiciens* (fig. 67) form a blue-black block, and the only other colours, apart from the light ground, are those of the shirt-fronts and instruments. Léger's dancers and acrobats would lead him to another theme, to a formal study which he would carry out over a period of several years: the *Plongeurs*.

Léger had the idea for the *Plongeurs* in Marseille in 1940, just before he went into exile. He saw a number of men swimming in a dock. The impression they made on him was vividly revived by the sight of a swimming pool in the United States: 'There weren't four or five divers; there were two hundred of them all at once. You could not tell who the heads, legs and arms belonged to. You could not make them out. So I put scattered limbs into my painting, and I realized that in doing that I was being much more truthful than Michelangelo when he took such pains over every muscle' (*L'Intérieur de l'art*, p. 75). It may or may not be the case that Michelangelo was being less 'truthful', but it is true that Léger was moving towards the same type of compactness. In *Plongeurs sur fond jaune* (1941, fig. 102), Léger retains some of the effects of the crowded large compositions of 1935–1939. Black masses with pseudopodia replace the clouds, and more angular forms replace the background elements. The small polychromatic details are now women's hair. The great innovation is the contrast between the clusters of human beings, which are still vaguely ochre or blue, and the patches of bright colour that fill the painting. In

503. 1943. Oil on canvas, 37 × 26 in. (94 × 66 cm). Galerie Louise Leiris, Paris.

Plongeurs II (1941–1942, fig. 104), all the bodies are painted in grisaille, and the hair is also grey, but the colour, which has broken free, now tends to take the form of interweaving irregular bands beneath the bodies. Everthing is in the centre of the canvas. In 1942, the human blocks of divers or dancers are simply drawn, and colour is flatly applied in broad autonomous areas, as in *La Danse* (fig. 100).

The divorce between drawing and colour appears in 1942, and Léger would exploit it on a more or less regular basis until the end of his life. It merits a digression. In a number of paintings executed in previous years (*Etude pour la composition aux perroquets* of 1934, for example), colour tended to escape the contours of the drawing; it is also likely that the indefinable shapes that might be interpreted as clouds in many of the paintings done in the 1930s (*Composition aux trois figures* or *Adam et Eve*, figs. 79 and 94) are as much the result of this intuition as of the need for a splash of colour outside the representational drawing. Léger was thus quite prepared for an important experience which he often described: 'When I was in New York in 1942, I was very struck by the advertizing spotlights that sweep the streets around Broadway. You are there talking to someone, and all at once he turns blue. Then the colour changes, another colour moves in front of the spotlight, and he turns red or yellow. That kind of colour, the colour of the spotlights, is free; it exists in space. I wanted to do the same thing in my canvases' (*L'Intérieur de l'art*, p. 73). From this point onwards, it is not unusual to find Léger executing two variants on a single painting: one with 'outside' colours, and one which is more conventional. In some cases, the drawing (*Les Trapézistes*, 1943) or a mass of bodies modelled in grisaille is all that remains on the canvas (*Les Acrobates en gris*, 1942–44, fig. 101). In general, Léger preferred ambiguity to systematic solutions; in the very fine *Plongeurs polychromes* (1942–1946, fig. 103) and in *Nature morte aux deux poissons* (1948, fig. 112), the colour is sometimes 'outside' and sometimes applied to the forms themselves. In that sense, *Adieu New York* (1946, fig. 110) is probably the masterpiece of the period because the painting juxtaposes the two methods of applying colour, and is at the same time a critique of its theme. Léger admired American cities and American technology. He liked their bright colours and their good natured pragmatism. America, much more so than Europe, gave him an intense vision of how objects can harmonize with natural elements — look at how, in 1943-1944, he contrasts the rounded, almost human forms of the flowers and trunks with the straight lines and sharp angles of the flat objects in *L'Arbre dans l'échelle* (fig. 108), or in the mysterious *503* (p. 23). But although he had sung the praises of this modern world, he finally realised that consumerism also leads to waste. Discussing *Adieu New York* with Pierre Descargues, he remarked: 'The USA is a country with countless rubbish dumps. Rather than repair anything, they throw everything away. Look, you can see mounds of scrap iron, parts of machines and even ties' (*Arts*, no. 147, 2 January 1948). The rubbish is juxtaposed against an enormous tree trunk which is rounded and modelled in blue-grey, just like the human bodies Léger was painting at this time. Did Léger now have less faith in manufactured objects? Great beams of light sweep in front of everything, over everything and behind everything, and bright luminous splashes cover the canvas. All that remained to be done was to add some foliage and a streamer bearing a somewhat nostalgic inscription. When he first visited New York in 1931, Léger had saluted 'the apotheosis of mechanical life'. His outbursts of optimism were sometimes clouded by doubts. 'The shapes of unknown machines. Eighteen chimneys all in a row, a gigantic organ. It's majestic and definitive. What confidence — what finish. The apotheosis of the machine. Is it an end in itself? I open a newspaper, and see the grimacing and emaciated face of Ghandi looking at me. Coincidence...' But his enthusiasm won the day: 'You should never get angry with a train that blows your hat off as it rushes by at a hundred miles an hour' (*Mes Voyages*, Paris: EFR, 1960, pp. 69, 56). Fifteen years later — including six years of war — *Adieu New York* and its rubbish tips did not look like a major aesthetic change, but it did at least denote a more circumspect view of the technological progress that had once inspired the young Léger.

A Painter Among Architects

The confined atmosphere of the studio was not enough for Fernand Léger. He had always been a man who was involved in life. He needed to go out into the streets, the factories and the villages, to be among people and to be part of the movement of modern life. He was not interested in being an observer, and wanted his artistic vocation to be as fully involved as possible in modern life. To his great regret, painting, unlike film which is in principle accessible to all and not only to a privileged elite, did not have the ability to reach very large numbers of people — a painting is unique, whereas many prints of the same film can be reproduced. Fortunately, a few film-makers and architects understood his ambitions and involved him in their reflection and their work.

His film sets and the designs for the Ballets Suédois brought Léger face to face with the problems inherent in reconciling painting and architecture.

Léger met the painter and architect Le Corbusier in 1920. Amédée Ozenfant and Le Corbusier, writing under the name Edouard Jeanneret, had already launched *purism* in their book *Après le cubisme* (1918), and they had just founded *L'Esprit nouveau*, a journal intended to promote everything in the literary and artistic world that related to their ideas.

Léger had for some time been looking for a way to free painting from the easel. He always cited *La Ville* (1919, fig. 29) as his first work to succeed in doing so, not because it depicted apartment blocks, staircases and other archictetural elements, but because it was painted with flat expanses of pure colour. The 'liberation' of colour was a precondition for any further research. At the same time, architects throughout the western world were attempting to do away with centuries of what they saw as superfluous ornamentation. 'The decorative hotchpotch that began with the Italian Renaissance', wrote Léger 'is a decadent phenomenon which has persisted in bourgeois art right down to our day' (*Variétés*, no. 10, 15 February 1929, p. 524). Those who had to live with them sometimes found blank whitewashed walls unbearable; architects therefore soon thought of using colour. But they were thinking of a very sparing use of colour to avoid a return to the over-decorated walls of the past.

Mural painting had never been abandoned, but the few painters to have practiced it on any scale — Puvis de Chavannes and, more recently Marcel-Lenoir and, more recently still, Torres-Garcia — had been satisfied with the spaces they were given and never questioned the contemporary relationship between painting and architecture. It was not until after the war that Severini, Delaunay and Herbin expressed a real desire to work in collaboration with architects. And only Léger combined his aesthetic reflections on easel-painting, with reflections on society: 'The advent of geometric towns, the advent of mechanical life, the manufactured object — absolute, hard, permanent, plastic and beautiful in its own right. A visual spectacle constantly transformed by the art of the window display. The modern street — aggressive, dazzling — posters, typographic letters. The geometric form is dominant. Its penetration into every domain, its visual and psychological influence… Imagine a town that is visually organized through the correct distribution of coloured values. Colour, an element of prime necessity, colour as social function' (*7 Arts*, no. 20, March 15, 1923). Léger returned to the same topic the following year, but in more specific terms: 'The world of work, the only interesting one, exists in an intolerable environment. Let us go into the factories, the banks, the hospitals. If light is required there, what does it illuminate? Nothing. Let's bring in colour: it is as necessary as water and fire. Let's apportion it wisely, so that it may be a more pleasant value, a psychological value; its moral influence can be considerable. A beautiful and calm environment. Life through colour… The polychromed hospital… A society without frenzy, calm, ordered, knowing how to live naturally within the Beautiful without exclamation or romanticism' (*Functions of Painting*, pp. 46–47). But only the most advanced architects understood the broad vision behind this profession of faith. Le Corbusier saw it as an appeal from a painter who was ahead of most architecture: 'This painting is architecture's sister. That is its contribution… The link is such and so imperative that of all the painters who are working today, Léger is the one whose paintings demand a new architecture. His paintings demand a contemporary setting that is in keeping with it and born of the same circumstances' (*Cahiers d'art*, no. 3-4, Paris, 1933). It was in this spirit that Le Corbusier and Robert Mallet-Stevens asked Léger to contribute something to their pavilions at the 1925 Exposition des Arts Décoratifs. The artist was probably not very satisfied with a painting like *Le Balustre* (fig. 61) placed on a wall in the *Esprit Nouveau* pavilion. Its sobriety was of course perfectly in keeping with the absence of embellishment and the simple lines of Le Corbusier's rooms and furniture, but it served the conventioal purpose of any framed canvas in any context: it was hung on the wall. Working on Mallet-Steven's *Pavillion d'un Ambassade* was a much more interesting proposition. Léger thought of a painting of specific dimensions for a specific setting (above the entrance). It was not framed, seemed to have been painted directly on the wall and, more important, its conception was also unusual for Léger. Being intended to highlight its surroundings rather than to draw the eye, it is a rigorously abstract composition of orthogonal planes, and is painted in more muted tones than those normally

used by the painter. In 1924–1925, Léger painted several *Compositions murales*, again using principles reminiscent of the De Stijl group in Holland (who, like the Russian constructivists, took a much bolder stance on combining painting and architecture). Léger had great respect for the approach taken by Mondrian and De Stijl, but he still had his doubts about their painting on the grounds that it did too much to encourage aestheticism. On the other hand, he always argued that abstract painting was particularly well suited to murals: 'I believe and I maintain that abstract art is in trouble when it tries to do easel painting. But for the mural the possibilities are unlimited' (*Functions of Painting*, p. 32). The difference between his mural experiments and his more or less representational easel-paintings is not in fact all that great; in both cases, Léger remains impersonal — it is extremely unusual for his figures or landscapes to be recognizable. And that impersonality was particularly well-suited to a 'machine for living' that could, like the Esprit Nouveau pavilion or Mallet-Stevens's public building, be reproduced in an infinite number of copies. Wilhelm Uhde, a shrewd contemporary observer, noticed this: 'Fernand Léger's paintings have a unique beauty: their inner grandeur. They do not stoop to meeting the needs of individual people, they rise above personal contingencies. I could just see them in a laboratory, a hospital or a school' (*Picasso et la tradition française*, Paris: Les Quatre-Chemins, 1928, p. 69). Although the comment is pertinent, it still leaves the painter in a

L'Échelle (Ladder). 1934–1935. Ink on paper, 14 1/8 × 10 7/8 in. (36 × 27.5 cm).

supporting role — rather as though he were there to fulfil the legal requirement that one per cent of the cost of constructing a public building in France must be spent on art, which usually results in the last-minute inclusion of a work of art that is quite out of place. A way out of this impasse had to be found. Over the next few years Léger thought about this problem constantly as he waited for suitable commissions, which rarely came his way.

The Brussels Exposition Internationale des Beaux-Arts of 1935 finally gave Léger the opportunity to decorate a gymnasium. The painter filled the spaces allotted to him with motifs inspired by sport — balls, weights, gynmastic apparatus, etc. He was conciliatory and did not interfere with things that did not concern him: 'Everything must be done harmoniously, with appopriate relationships; the architect's power must not be diminished, and his desire to destroy the wall or simply have an accompaniment to the all must be taken into account' (*Functions of Painting*, p. 186). Basically, on this occasion the painter can have done little more than make a minor contribution to the overall conception, as the best architects were not yet accustomed to collaborating with artists in any real sense (and mediocre architects will never get used to doing so). And yet the whole era was preoccupied with the need for collective art. In 1935-1936 a wide ranging but rather oddly-named 'debate over realism' was launched by the Maison de la Culture.

In order to understand the so-called debate and Léger's position, we have to remember the intellectual and social context. As a result of the political clashes between left and right and of the public demonstrations that so violently divided public opinion in the 1930s in the wake of revolutions and counter-revolutions — the Bolshevik revolution was giving way to Stalinism and the first Moscow trials, fascism was triumphant in Italy and Nazism in Germany, while social agitation was soon to turn to tragedy in Spain — a number of intellectuals were trying to establish relations with 'the people'. Some writers renounced avant-gardism in favour of a so-called 'populist', popular or simply realist literature. They then found themselves exposed to the ridicule of the supporters of the supposedly more difficult or innovatory tradition of Joyce and Proust or surrealism. But it was in the visual arts that positions were most clear-cut. In 1935, the Communist-inspired journal *Commune* organized a survey on 'Where is Painting Going?' The artists consulted belonged to different generations and different tendencies, but the one thing they had in common was that they were all, to a greater or lesser extent, figurative artists: Jean Lurçat, Marcel Gromaire, Robert Delaunay, André Derain, Frans Masereel, Max Ernst, Raoul Dufy, Christian Bérard, and André Lhote ostentatiously ignored abstraction. The abstract artists had united under the banner of 'Abstraction-Creátion', a vast association which organised exhibitions and publications and brought together leading French and foreign painters like Kandinsky, Mondrian, Kupka, Herbin,

Arp, Brancusi, Ben Nicholson, Freundlich, Schwitters, Wadsworth, Vantongerloo, and dozens of others. The debate over realism was directed against them. Picasso and Matisse kept out of the fray, but the supporters of realism were only too ready to invoke their authority. The position of the surrealist painters was more ambiguous; some were asked for their views, but they did not take part in the following year's debates at the Maison de la Culture, and surrealism was either ignored or condemned by the participants because, like the abstract painters, the surrealists made no attempt to express 'social realities'. Everyone — Gromaire, Aragon, Léger, Le Corbusier, Lurçat and Lhote — agreed that the Popular Front was a time for realism. The need for a realist art was in fact the only thing they did agree about; the content they gave it varied so much that their positions were sometimes mutually exclusive. Aragon's 'socialist realism', which was to be the motor behind the transformation of society, had little in common with Le Corbusier's realism, which included abstract art: 'In terms of international production, so-called French abstract art is concrete. It is essentially concrete. Realism is internal' (*La Querelle du réalisme*, Paris: Cercle d'Art, 1987, p. 116). Being as much an architect as a painter, Le Corbusier obviously took a social or philosophical view, and not an academic view, of the visual arts. His collaborator Léger obviously shared his point of view. In the first lecture he gave in 1913, he had insisted that 'The realistic value of a work of art is completely independent of any imitative character' (*Functions of Painting*, p. 3). In 1936, he again stated that: 'Realisms vary because the artist is living in a different period, in a new environment and a general intellectual climate which dominates and influences his mind' (*La Querelle du réalisme*, p. 103). Léger's realism was not an imitation or a copy of the real world. Look at a few canvases from this period: *Composition à l'aloès No. 3* (1935, fig. 85), *La Fleur polychrome* (1936, fig. 83) and *Le Grand coq bleu* (1937, fig. 92). Anyone who denies that these are realist paintings is adopting what Léger called 'the ape's point of view' — and 'aping' reality is of no comtemporary interest. There would be a renewal of interest in these questions after the war, but for the moment they led Léger and Le Corbusier to concentrate on the problem of a collectively conceived community art: 'The collaboration between mural painting, statuary and architecture envisaged here requires discipline, specific qualities of monumentality and considerable preparation' (*La Querelle du réalisme*, p. 122). Léger was nostalgic for the days when anonymous artists could paint or create mosaics on a wall for all to use. The Renaissance saw the birth of individualism and capitalism, and that of easel painting. Paintings could be transported and sold. They became the personal property of wealthy collectors and museums, and the majority suffered as a result. Art became divorced from the people. Because they had no time and no education, argued Léger, the people had no access to art: their tastes were forced upon them by their rudimentary education (talk of counter-education through the media was still a thing of the future) or by a demagogic *ouvrièrisme*. A quantitative view of work and imitation — the ape's point of view — were therefore their only criteria. 'Fight for your leisure, your freedom; you are right', cried Léger. 'Once those freedoms have been acquired, you will be able to cultivate yourselves, to develop your sensitivity, and to appreciate the beauty and newness of the modern arts' (*Functions of Painting*, p. 130). He proposed a a whole program of reforms: 'They ought to begin in grade school. Children ought to be surrounded by beautiful objects and beautiful pictures, so that when they become adults their artistic formation will be much easier. Children's drawings are generally beautiful, and are always very inventive. Children do not copy nature' (ibid., p. 125). These are the words of a generous man. As he waited for public walls to be made available to him, Léger lectured in workers' clubs, exhibited without much success in factories, and worked at his easel.

The French State was no longer in the habit of giving artists public commissions — but at the same time, to Léger's envy, Mexican artists were working full-time on commissions. It took an exceptional event like the International Arts et Techniques exhibition of 1935 for France to offer commissions to Léger, Delaunay, Herbin, Dufy, Survage and dozens of other artists. Some twelve painters were commissioned to decorate Mallet-Steven's Pavillon de la Solidarité Nationale. Only Delaunay's panel did not clash with Léger's. Maurice Denis's crowd at the fountain and even Gromaire's harvesters looked terribly fussy when compared with Léger's schematic shovels and hammers interlaced with ropes. When he was asked what contribution he would like to make to the fair, Léger expressed the wish that that all the unemployed should be taken on to whitewash the facades of Paris's apartment blocks and that the different areas of the fair itself should be painted in very bright colours. His ideas were thought somewhat alarming. In 1931 he had imagined a glass New York : 'A transparent, translucent New York, with blue, yellow and red floors! An unprecedented fairyland, the light unleashed by Edison streaming through all that and pulverizing the buildings' (*Functions of Painting*, p. 88). All this sounded absurd. Léger was, however, given responsibility for a vast mural for the Palais de la Découverte. The result was *Le Transport des forces* (fig. 87): angular structures of girders and stylised factories against the supple, curved forms of the natural elements. Still within the context of the fair, Léger designed the sets and costumes for a project that meant a great deal to him: Jean-Richard Bloch's play *Naissance d'une cité*, with music by Milhaud and Honegger. The play had in fact been in preparation since 1933. A manifesto issued by 'Spéctacles d'équipe' suggested exploring ways to allow 'a collective recognition of the conditions for an art that can pool the resources of the theatre and the resources of the stadium' (*Léger och Norden*, p. 75). Each of the five performances was seen by ten thousand people. A working-class audience for a play at the Vélodrome d'Hiver! Léger was delighted.

Exhilarating though they may have been, these large-scale works were not permanent. In 1939, there was talk of a commission for a popular flying club near Nancy. Léger executed a whole series of gouaches and oils and a maquette for the planned mural (1940, fig. 96), all on the theme of an aeroplane in the sky. The defeat of 1940 put an end to the project, and in October Léger went into exile in the United States. He did, however, rework his maquette and turn it into a painting: *L'Avion dans le ciel* (1939–1952, fig. 95). The work is completely abstract, but it still has a suprisingly figurative look. Irregular blue, green and brown shapes float above a surface. They could be either clouds or sculptures by Arp or Moore. They intersect three elements which the viewer is quite happy to leave unidentified, and highlight the background motif of a large disk made up of red, white and blue concentric circles. Is it an aeroplane reduced to the movement of its propeller? A roundel? A target? The sun? It does not matter. The canvas is beautiful. The fresco would have been magnificent.

Fernand Léger spent the five years of the war in the United States, convinced that 'nothing important could happen in painting during a modern war' (*La Querelle du réalisme*, p. 226). Although he made his living by teaching in various institutions, he continued to work on his old projects and to begin new ones. There is no break between the two. He went back to the motifs of the musicians and acrobats of the 1920s and 1930s, but painted them in his new style, applying colour outside the drawings and contrasting them with his new themes (cyclists, for example). But he was still obsessed by the idea of a large public painting. He approached officials and patrons. In late 1942, he wrote to the director of New York's Museum of Modern Art: 'My present wish would be too, to find one wall to realise the "Men in the space" in the technic of the picture, which one, I believe, interest you [*sic*]. Can you help me to find this wall? It is not for me a purpose of money. I have never been very preoccupied with this question. I would now like to realise a big mural painting which would be the culminating of my two years work in the USA. One University's wall, one college, the White House, Sing Sing!! Why not? Think of it. You are, I believe, admirable in place for that [*sic*]. I shall be very grateful to you' (*Léger's Le Grand Déjeuner*, p. 71). There were a number of projects, but none of them came to anything. Léger did not, however, lose hope, particularly as he had met Father Couturier, a Dominican who had once studied with Maurice Denis and who was enamoured of painting. Father Couturier had no difficulty in convincing Léger that, once peace returned, postwar reconstruction would make everything possible, especially in religious art — a domain in which he expected to see a renaissance.

When Fernand Léger returned to France at the end of 1945, he had greater hopes than ever that a society in which life would be more just and more pleasant would emerge

Bolivar. 1950. Opéra de Paris, Tableau II, scene 3.

Mosaïque et céramique murales (Mosaic and Ceramic Mural). 1955 Gaz de France, Alfortville.

from the ruins of the war. He joined the Communist Party — which Picasso had joined a year earlier — in a fit of fraternity. In the immediate post-war years, the construction industry put first things first, and had litle time to worry about aesthetics. Léger did not receive any official commissions. As in the past, his only commissions were for ballets and operas (Prokoviev's *Le Pas d'Acier* in 1948, and Supervielle and Milhaud's *Bolivar* in 1949: p. 28). Father Couturier did, however, ask him to design a fifty-square metre mosaic for the church in Assy (Haute Savoie). Some surprise was expressed that an atheist painter should agree to portray the Virgin; Gino Severini, a Masaicist comrade, raised the more serious objection that the mosaic lacked fervour. In his view, the great face in the centre of the mosaic was no more than 'another of Léger's heads with rays of light around it. That's all there is to it' (*La Querelle du réalisme*, p. 298). Leger himself wanted his mural to have more significance than a religious effigy over the door of a Catholic church: it should be 'a temple for contemplation' (*Functions of Painting*, p. 46). As for the criticism that his faces were stereotyped, it has to be remembered that he regarded facial features and expressions as purely anecdotal; the few portraits he left — the 1931 *Portrait de madame Dale* and the portraits of *Henri Martin* and *Mayakovsky* that he executed twenty years later — are not usually very convincing. Léger saw himself as a descendent of the pre-Renaissance painters of frescoes and mosaics, and they had shown little concern for the diversity or the psychological expressions of the people they depicted. This is a constant throughout Fernand Léger's work.

From the 1950s onwards, Léger enjoyed worldwide fame. Painters were now beginning to receive public commissions, and he had the oportunity to work for the community as much as for collectors. He produced mosaics for the crypt of the American War Memorial in Bastogne (1950), stained glass and tapestries for the church in Audincourt (1950–1951), decorations for the large auditorium of the United Nations building in New York (1952), stained-glass windows for the church in Courfaivre, Switzerland (1953–1954), and stained glass windows for the University of Caracas (1954). Many of his maquettes were not executed until after his death: the ceramic and mosaic mural for Gaz de France's administrative building in Alfortville, the mosaic for the Sao Paolo opera house, the monumental ceramics for the *jardin d'enfants* and the façade of the Musée Fernand Léger in Biot, the mosaics for the Memorial Hospital in Saint-Lo… 'I have always dreamed of large mural surfaces … It does not matter if it is the wall of a church or a school' (Cited, Brassaï, *Les Artistes de ma vie*, Paris: Denoel, 1982, p. 94).

It is noticeable that Léger was now using a greater range of techniques. In the nave of the church designed by the architect Maurice Novarina in Audincourt, Léger set seventeen stained-glass windows in concrete, using the *dalle-de-verre* technique. They set the nave ablaze with light. Léger approached the objects of the Passion — cups, whips, ropes and swords — with the same fascination he had always felt for objects, and did not have to make any concessions to achieve his stated aim of 'doing as much as possible to bring out their magic.' His windows are surely one of the masterpieces of modern stained glass, and even his severe friend Severini declared himself to be satisfied with them. In 1949, Léger studied ceramics with his old pupil Roland Brice. Using this new technique, he executed reliefs like *Femmes au perroquet* (1952, fig. 37) and sculptures like the dazzling *Fleur polychrome* (1952, fig. 130). He wanted these sculptures to be displayed in squares and parks, and not in museums. The most colossal of his ceramics is the *jardin d'enfants* in Biot (fig. 136): an assemblage of several very brightly coloured and non-representational structures on which children are allowed to climb and play, in accordance with Léger's wishes. He sometimes combined different techniques. High up on the Gaz de France façade in Alfortville, a ceramic relief depicting a burning bush is set into a brightly-coloured abstract mosaic. Similarly, two black and white reliefs representing arms playing with a ball and a figure with a bicycle, stand out against the brightly-coloured mosaic motifs on the façade of the museum in Biot (fig. 137) — it is somehow reminiscent of Gaudí's fantastic art, and in his *Mes Voyages* Léger speaks very openly of his admiration for the Catalan architect, whose work he discovered when he was travelling with Le Corbusier in 1930.

A Painter Among the People

The first post-war decade saw a revival in religious art which reached its apotheosis with Matisse's chapel in Vence (1948–1951), Le Corbusier's church in Ronchamp and, of course, Léger's church in Audincourt, but it must not be forgotten that this was also the period of socialist realism in both art and literature. The era was marked by the tensions of the cold war, which had cut the world in two: two Germanys with a wall between them, and two Koreas with a war (1950–1953) between them. American consumer goods were as seductive, albeit in a different way, as Stalin's propaganda, and a Europe devastated by war therefore became all the more divided. In the United States, Senator MacCarthy was leading a witch hunt against everything that was deemed 'Un-American' in the cultural world; in the USSR Andrei Zdhanov was repressing everything that did not conform to socialist realism. French Communists followed his orders. 'The Party has an aesthetic', wrote Aragon in 1946, 'and it is called realism.' Not everything was that simple; even in Communist circles there were objections to slogans about realism, and none of the 'big three' — Matisse, Picasso and Léger — obeyed them. Herbin protested against realism (1949), and abstraction was already beginning to gain ground.

How did Léger, man and artist, find himself in such a Manichaean context? He took sides as a citizen — he was a communist — but it is very rare to find any obvious sign of his commitment in his art. Why didn't Léger, who is often regarded as being somewhat naive, paint portraits of Stalin and *Massacres en Corée*, as Picasso did? He did in fact draw a portrait of the Rosenbergs, who were condemned to death in 1951 for spying on behalf of the USSR, but that was very much the exception to the rule. He felt indebted to the United States and still had a great deal of sympathy for that country. He did not believe that art should obey slogans: 'As for these recent manifestations of rushed paintings of political subjects dreamed up for reasons that have nothing to do with artistic concerns, they are of no interest' (*Pour un réalisme du XXe siècle*, p. 143). Neither Léger nor Picasso took part in the 1952 debate about realism. 1936 was gone. They had to be left to get on with their own work, whether people liked it or not. No one dared to object to the time Léger was spending in churches. He had never concealed his liking for Romanesque and Gothic art, but, what was more important, he saw it as an opportunity to work outside the context of galleries and museums. He was quite unconcerned about working on behalf of a religion he did not believe in, provided that it allowed people to experience the pleasure they gained from any other beautiful spectacle. 'Possessing wonderful churches [the Catholic religion], has pushed the art of the spectacle very far; it has subjugated the masses, through masterly and deliberate direction of its interior and exterior cult manifestations... If it has imposed itself on the world, that is because it has not neglected any of the visual and auditory means of its epoch' (*Functions of*

Levers de rideau sur la question du bonheur (The Curtain Rises on the Question of Happiness). 1955. Design for book cover, 12 ⁵/₈ x 9 ¹/₂ in. (32 × 24 cm).

Painting, p. 36). If we fail to take into account both his independence and his acute sense of fraternity, we will not understand Léger.

Although he was committed to his art and committed to people, Léger had no doctrinal commitments. He never wanted art to be available only to the usual audience of collectors and professionals. He dreamed of art for all. In the 1930s, he somewhat naively tried to exhibit his work in factories; he was no more successful fifteen years later. At best, people became used to seeing them in the canteen and usually judged them in purely representational terms. 'It is true that, in order to enjoy art, you have to have a certain culture and an education; you have to have time, and so long as people have to work until seven in the evening, it is impossible to do anything' (*L'Intérieur de l'art*, p. 85). Léger was, however, still convinced that factory and office workers 'have a capacity for admiration and enthusiasm that can be sustained and developed in the direction of modern painting' (*Functions of Painting*, p. 135), and that they simply had to be given time and education.

At this point, a digression is needed. Léger taught for almost the whole of life, not so much for financial reasons as because of his desire to be directly useful, to be involved in an exchange from which he too could gain something. Between 1924 and 1931, he taught at the Académie Moderne with Othon Frisz, Alexandra Exter and Ozenfant, and from 1935 until the outbreak of war at the Académie d'art Contemporain, which he founded. He also taught during his years of exile in the United States. From 1946 until his death, he taught at the Atelier Fernand Léger. At the Atelier, no distinction was made between nationalities ('Nationalism in art is superficial', he wrote in 1932, 'You have to take the beautiful where you find it, without worrying about the signature', *Léger och Norden*, p. 69) or tendencies ('the diversity of tendencies — abstraction, surrealism, figuration — and the variety of techniques was proof of the absolute

Groupe de musiciens (Group of Musicians). 1925. Pencil, 8 ¼ × 10 ⅝ in. (21 × 27 cm).

freedom that Léger wanted to preserve' (Georges Bauquier, in *Fernand Léger*, 1956, p. 20). In 1929, Léger introduced advertising and related subjects into the curriculum of his painting academy. He liked to say that he had produced more poster-designers, photographers and window-dressers than conventional artists. That may well be true, but who can forget that his students included Otto Carlsund, Tarsila do Amaral, Marcelle Cahn, Erik Olson, Franciska Clausen, Florence Henri, Arpad Szenes, Veira da Silva, Marek Wlodarski, Nicolas de Stael, Richard Stankiewicz, Sam Francis, William Klein, Aurélie Nemours…?

It is possible, if we try hard enough, to relate certain of Léger's works — *Les Constructeurs* (fig. 140) is quite rightly the most famous — to the prevailing *ouvrièrisme* of the 1950s. *Ouvrièrisme* was a reaction to the rise of informal art and the return of surrealism, but it should not be forgotten that Léger himself denounced its inherent demagogy and had been celebrating the solidarity and straightforward camaraderie of the world of work for decades. Ever since the woodcutters of his *Nus dans la forêt* of 1909—1910, he had painted countless mechanics, typographers, drivers and people from the world of entertainment and countless views of factories, not to mention leisure-pursuits like dancing and fishing. Léger was not concerned with 'class art'. *La Partie des cartes* (1917) depicts soldiers and officers playing cards and smoking; there are three of them. The figures in the various versions of *Les Trois Musiciens* painted between 1925 and 1944 are discreetly differentiated by the clothes they wear: the bare-headed accordionist wears the striped jersey of a sailor or a worker. The man playing the saxhorn (or tuba) is always more middle-class, and wears a waistcoat, a bowler hat and a bow tie in the 1930 version (fig. 67), and a tie, a trilby and a rosette in the 1944 version. The elegant cellist (who may in fact be playing a double bass; realistic accuracy was not one of Léger's concerns) who had a boater and a stiff collar in 1930 has became somewhat less fashionable by 1944: his wing collar and flannel belt suggest that he is a peasant — and Léger greatly admired peasant dress. Once again, there are three figures, as in the *Trois Camarades* of 1920 (fig. 37) and the *Trois soeurs* of 1952 (fig. 127). Léger attached great value to the number three. In his view, it was, both *instinctively* and *harmoniously*, a lucky number: '3, a vital, balanced number, as opposed to the romantic, abstract 2. Life in all its manifestations, whatever they may be, becomes orderly, harmonious and lasting when they are found in uneven numbers. The figure 2 is black and white — vertical — horizontal. 3 has the same qualities, plus another quite indefinable quality, a grey value — but it is an essential part of rhythm and movement… 3 is an in-betweenart' (*Mes Voyages*, p. 134). This may not have been true for anyone but the artist; if we read it carefully, the statement is, however, more than just an explanation of the forms and colours of his *Trois musiciens*.

It was in this state of mind that Léger resolved to go back to what he called 'the great subject'. He did not mean

Les **Constructeurs** (Construction Workers). 1951. Couverture en couleurs, 5 5/8 × 9 in. (14.3 × 22.8 cm). Coloured book jacket.

Les **Constructeurs** (Builders). 1951. Colour lithograph, 5 5/8 × 9 in. (14.3 × 22.8 cm).

Nelson at Trafalgar or Apollo driving his chariot, but something 'everyone can understand' — another of his favourite expressions. This certainly did not mean a return to an edifying or committed art. Léger was aware that, in a period when everyone could read, listen to the radio and go to the cinema, the role of the modern painter was not, as it had been in the Middle Ages, to supply documentary, pedagogic or propaganda images — other media could do that better. The artist was now freed from all bookish tasks: 'The book frees Art and makes possible Art for Art's sake, an escape from reality. The imagination becomes primary, and the subject is no more than a means' (*Functions of Painting*, p. 161). He displays an astonishing independence and self-awareness for a painter working in 1950. His great public paintings — *Les Loisirs*, *Les Constructeurs*, *La Partie de campagne* — explain nothing, demonstrate nothing and exist only to give the viewer pleasure, just like his more difficult works. It is significant that when, in 1951, he unveiled his *Les Constructeurs* at the Maison de la Pensée Française, which was a communist-inspired popular cultural centre, Léger included an abstract lithograph (p. 31) in the presentation copies of the book published to coincide with the exhibition.

Léger made his intentions clear, not in words, but in a painting he had been thinking about for a long time: *Les Loisirs* (1948-1949, fig. 114). The idea for the painting presumably predates *La Grande Julie* of 1945 (fig. 109), which depicts a woman with a bicycle and wearing sports clothes, and presumably goes back to the period when Léger was demanding 'leisure' for all. Leisure for all became a reality with the Popular Front legislation on paid holidays and compulsory weekly rest days, and with the subsequent mass exodus into the countryside and the suburbs — which were still green. *Les Loisirs* is so obviously based on memories of the days of the Popular Front that the early version of 1944-1945 — a frontal view of the four men sitting, standing and leaning on a bicycle — is actualy entitled *La Belle Equipe* (p. 31). Julien Duvivier's film *Le Belle Equipe* was made in 1936 — the year in which Jean Renoir made *Une Partie de campagne*. It is in that film that we hear Jean Gabin singing to a suitably worthy group of proletarians: '*Quand on se promène au bord de l'eau... Les petits oiseaux...*' ('When you walk by the water's edge... The little birds...').

Habits did not change greatly between the pre-war period and the early 1950s. 'Leisure' consisted mainly of

Les **Cyclistes** (Cyclists). 1950. Ink and gouache on blue-grey paper, 18 7/8 × 24 5/8 in. (48 × 62.5 cm). Musée National d'Art Moderne, Centre Georges Pompidou, Paris

La **Belle Equipe**. 1944. Ink on paper, 15 × 22 in. (38 × 56 cm). Galerie Louis Carré, Paris.

going for outings. If one went for a walk — and people walked a lot in those days — one wore one's Sunday best — suit and tie — and boaters were still worn. In order go on country outings and really to get away from the town and its habits, the fortunate few had carefully maintained pre-war bangers, and the rest used the indispensable bicycle. A young, sporty look was fashionable, and mothers and aunts wore divided skirts, shorts or baggy trousers. My mother had a striped knitted bathing costume, just like the woman cyclist, and I had yellow rompers, just like those worn by the child on the luggage-carrier, but mine had a butterfly on the front and not a star. And off we went. We met people. We went fishing and swimming. We picked flowers beneath the trees and the fences (and the electricity pylons). We went to see the sea, and to watch the cyclists in the Tour de France, *les petits oiseaux...*

All this is captured in *Les Loisirs* (figs. 114, 115), *La Partie de campagne* and *Le Campeur* (figs. 132, 135). They capture a whole period. This is Léger's 'great subject' and it is the equal of any *Sacré de Napoléon*. The painting is representational and immediately comprehensible, but free: the improbable bicycles and birds cock a snook at realism. This is above all a visual composition which belongs within a specific tradition. In the best known version of *Les Loisirs* (fig. 114), the reclining woman is holding a newspaper in which we can read the words: *Hommage à Louis David*. The painting obviously postdates the David exhibition held in the Orangerie (June–September 1948), but Léger had long spoken of his admiration for David. It was, he recalled, the Douanier Rousseau who first took him to see David's paintings. And he later said: 'I feel that David is much closer to me than Michelangelo, especially when he paints portraits. I like the dryness in David's work, and in that of Ingrés' (*L'Intérieur de l'art*, p. 74). One does indeed think of David's clean portraits and of his vividly sketched figures; the leg of the woman in the divided skirt is excessively elongated to meet the requirements of the pictorial composition, and is reminiscent of Ingres's elongated odalisques; the massive horizontality of her leg balances the painting because it contrasts with the uprights of the standing figures and the curves of the wheels. One thinks of the Douanier Rousseau's group portraits, which are centred in similar fashion, with the impenetrable but happy figures seen facing us. One thinks of coloured images. One thinks of *Le Déjeuner sur l'herbe*, in which the pioneering brings the city into the countryside. One thinks. And one thinks most of all of Léger.

In a second, and perhaps more private, version of *Les Loisirs*, Léger simply puts a flower and not an inscription in the reclining woman's hand, and places the whole group against a very unrealistic red background. But the faces are still impassively serene and have scarcely any individuality. The great exception is *Les Constructeurs* (1955, fig. 124), in which the faces are diversified, and where the movements of the figures and the folds of their clothing are carefully delineated. As Leger explains, the reasons for this are purely formal: 'I tried to get the most violent contrasts by opposing human figures painted with scrupulous realism to the clouds and the metallic structures. I don't know whether I succeeded, but I think anyway it was a quarrel to provoke' (*Functions of Painting*, p. 182) Adopting a theme that was quite in keeping with this period of reconstruction, Léger deliberately follows the formal tradition to which he often referred: the contrast between architecture and human figures can be seen in primitives like Giotto, Uccello or Fra Angelico, but it can also be seen in Poussin (*L'Eucharistie*, *La Mort de Saphire* and *L'Enlèvement des Sabines*, which Leger admired), David (*Le Serment des Horaces* and *Brutus*) and in Ingres (*Odalisque à l'esclave*, *Antiochus et Stratonice*). Ever since the *Escalier* of 1913, Léger had often turned to this contrast. He used three elements to organize his composition: flat areas of paint and the angular lines of the metal ladders and scaffolds against the plain sky; almost non-representational curved elements (ropes, clouds); and more finely worked and modelled figures with complex forms. Various studies and smaller compositions (*Les Constructeurs à la chane*) show that Léger experimented with a horizontal composition before opting for the dynamic upward movement of the final large-format painting.

For a number of his late compositions, Léger experimented with many different variants and approaches. His exploration of a subject was a gradual process, as we can clearly see in the case of *La Partie de campagne* (1953–1954, figs. 134, 135). It is of course painted in the same spirit as *Les Loisirs*, but it owes still more to the tradition inaugurated by *Le Déjeuner sur l'herbe*, which the neo-impressionists had made their own; one thinks, for example, of Seurat's *La Baignade* or *Un Dimanche d'été à la Grande Jatte* or, in a more edifying register, of Signac's *Au Temps d'harmonie* and Matisse's more timeless *Luxe, calme et volupté* — Léger obviously felt more sympathy for the lack of sentimentality in the former. In the first version (coll. S. Hahn, New York), a trio of figures sit or recline on the grass and face the viewer; by the water in the background, a young boy and a fisherman casting his line turn their backs to the viewer (one thinks of Jean Renoir's *Partie de campagne*). In the second version (Musée Fernand Léger, Biot), the water has been moved into the foreground and the child and fishing rod have been replaced by a motor car; the fisherman, who is still in exactly the same position, becomes a man now opening the bonnet. There is an obvious similarity with *Le Campeur* (fig. 132) in which a woman with a bunch of flowers and a semi-reclining woman watch two children in the water (again, there are several versions dating from 1953–1954). There is also a squarer version (Museum Ludwig, Cologne) without the left-hand section and the fisherman/motorist. Only the trio and the two children in the water remain — this time the man is wearing a suit and the women are nude, as in Manet. In the great definitive version, the questions of costume and nudity disappear. Léger in fact reworks the drawing of the first version. He includes the car but not the children, but

Femme à l'oiseau sur fond rouge (Woman with Bird, Red Background). 1952. Oil on canvas, 36 ¼ × 28 ¾ in. (92 × 73 cm).

Composition murale sur fond jaune (Mural Composition on Yellow Background). 1952. 58 ¼ × 38 ⅝ in. (148 × 98 cm).

completely transforms the atmosphere by applying broad swathes of colour outside the drawing. A calm summer day thus becomes an explosion of sunlight, warmth and joy. Modern though it may be, the juxtaposition of black drawing and white figurative drawing (as in a posed holiday snapshot) and abstract painting, is also an extension of a process that could be found in old popular prints, where the match between the coloured stencil and the printed design is very approximate. Tradition combines with innovation.

A lot of time had passed since the days when Léger used to go to the Médrano circus with Apollinaire and Cendrars. *Le Cirque* (1918, fig. 26) was the first of many paintings of acrobats and dancers. The contortions that distort their bodies are of as much interest to Léger as the spangles, colours and lights they display; like Leger himself, his circus people had a liking for showy accessories and objects. And yet it took forty years for him to elaborate *La Grande parade* (fig. 133), which was to be his great pictorial testament. As always, Léger worked slowly and in stages. His acrobats and dancers were always rounded, but it was in about 1948, with a series that includes *L'Acrobate et sa partenaire* (fig. 113), that the idea of movement begins to take shape: a centrifugal force propels the acrobat and bends his limbs until they are as rounded as the ring-target in whose centre he is performing. 'Nothing is as round as the circus. It is an

enormous bowl in which circular forms unroll. Nothing stops, everything is connected. The ring dominates, commands, absorbs. The audience is the moving scenery; it sways with the action in the ring. The faces are raised, lowered; they shout, laugh. The horse goes round, the acrobat shifts his position, the bear jumps through his hoop, and the juggler throws his rings into space. The circus is a rotation of masses, people, animals and objects' (*Functions of Painting*, p. 172). But Léger was primarily interested in the organization of his subject. Since 1950, he had been studying it with greater care than ever. He published *Le Cirque*, an album of sixty-three lithographs which is alive with people, objects and animals. He drew the jugglers, tumblers, trapeze artists, riders and clowns he needed for his great canvas. He looked for inspiration to earlier figures (*Marie l'acrobate*, and even *Adam et Eve*), and even thought for a moment of including his *Trois musiciens*. After numerous experiments, the drawing was finished in 1953: *La Grande Parade, Dessin fond rouge* (fig. 131). The drawing is all of a piece, as though it were glued to the red ground. Whereas Léger's figures once floated in space (*Les Trois Sœurs*, 1952, fig. 127) or were painted in grisaille (*Femme à l'oiseau sur fond rouge*, 1952, p. 33), the drawing is now flat and there is no depth or modelling effects. It should be noted that Léger did sometimes paint in black on the white ground of the canvas without adding any colour (the most intriguing of these experiments is probably the poem-painting *Les Mains des constructeurs* of 1951, which combines text and drawing). The ropes, apparatus, weights, balls, rings and all the marvelous paraphernalia of the circus have as much value as the figures and the horse. Léger appears to have retouched the drawing only when he executed the final 1954 version (fig. 133) and, as in *La Partie de Campagne*, he seems to have added large flat areas of abstract colour. If we look more closely, we can see that both the drawing and the colours are more complex than in the schema. The drawing is no longer flat; black shading emphasises the movement of the limbs and the roundness of the objects. Details that were carefully painted in will be either painted over or left to show through the bands of even colour that segment the picture. The eye is fascinated, absorbed and intrigued by the shifting relations between colour and line, both of which alternate between having two and three dimensions. A great red comet with a blue and orange tail shoots across a celebration of joyous life.

Léger's contemporaries were still debating the question of figuration and non-figuration, but he had long since moved on from those issues. *Composition murale sur fond jaune* (1952, fig. 330) is as completely abstract as the *Deux Papillons jaunes sur une échelle* (fig. 126) is joyously representational. Léger did not live long enough to sign his final work, *Composition aux deux oiseaux sur fond jaune* (fig. 138), which combines clouds in an exhilarating yellow sky, and indefinable angular and motionless still constructions. Two fantastic birds are at play in them. They are neither Gallic cocks, golden eagles, doves of peace nor the Holy Ghost. They are quite simply birds: beautiful birds speckled with grey. 'These works were executed with freedom and truth as his companions in arms; simply by observing the new realities that dominated his time. He saw them, felt them...' (F. L. Preface to P. Descargues, *Fernand Léger*, Paris: Cercle d'Art, 1955, p. 6).

In 1913, Apollinaire described Léger's work as an attempt to make people *happy*. As though to prove him right, Léger always painted his hopes for the future. It is because he was an optimist that he could define a painting as 'a condensed joy' to be shared by as many people as possible. He was ready to collaborate with industry and to encourage the applied arts in order to make the world more beautiful. People laughed when he dreamed of his coloured utopia, of polychrome and glass towns with lights shining through them. He believed that, when properly used, colour was a life-force and had healing properties. And yet even in 1924, he was not blind to the dangers of modernity in the city:

'The hypertension of contemporary life , its daily assault on the nerves, is due at least 40 per cent to the overdynamic exterior environment. The visual world of a large modern city, that vast spectacle... is badly orchestrated; in fact not orchestrated at all. The intensity of the street shatters our nerves and drives us crazy. Let's tackle the problem in all its scope. Let's organize the exterior spectacle. This is nothing more nor less than creating "polychromed architecture" from scratch and taking in all the manifestations of current advertizing. If the spectacle offers intensity, a street, a city, a factory ought to offer an obvious plastic intensity. Let's organize exterior life in its domain: form, colour, light' (*Functions of Painting*, p. 46). Léger never lost heart, not even in the face of the chaos and bad taste to be seen on the walls, in architecture and town planning, not even in the face of visual, aural and toxic pollution, or, in a word, of the city's ultimate lack of respect for man: 'It is disorder that is part of every revolution at the beginning. The time has come to try and bring some order to this anarchy, I believe' (Ibid., p. 186). His most prophetic words were spoken at the Sorbonne in 1934, when he lectured on the evolution of society 'From the Acropolis to the Eiffel Tower': 'A new *way* might be emerging. Normal values have been mocked too much. Everyone wanted to eat grapes in January and go skating in August. Is it so hard to wait?... Money and speculation have distorted everything with their gilded touch and their excessive speed. *Let's walk*. Let's look around us. Drive your car at 25mph wih the top down. Look to your left and your right. You will see that there are still trees, with birds in them. It's been a long time since anyone looked at a bird. No time. Remember that the great natural functions must be our barometer, despite everything ... Locomotives, aeroplanes and boats are going mad; we forget the predominant immobile strength of raw materials. We have to find a balance' (*Pour une reálisme du XIXe siècle*, pp. 237–138). Although he had no theories, ecological or otherwise, Léger was a painter-citizen who wanted to believe that common sense and fraternity would eventually prevail, provided that a few natural rules were remembered. Whether or not we share that belief, it is certainly a noble one. As is the other belief he expressed at various times, sometimes in connection with the basic humanism of even the simplest circus turn: 'An oak that can be destroyed in twenty seconds took a hundred years to grow. The birds are always marvelously dressed; progress is a word stripped of its meaning, and a cow that nourishes the world will always go two miles an hour' (*Functions of Painting*, p. 177). That is Léger's message. Anyone who takes the time to look at them can read it in his paintings.

Chronology

1881

Jules-Henri-Fernand Léger born in Argentan (Orne) on 4 February; his father, Henri-Armand Léger, dies in 1884; his mother, Marie-Adèle Daunou, in 1922. Attends school in Argentan, and subsequently in Tinchebray.

1897

Apprenticed to an architect in Caen; he will stay there until 1899.

1900

Moves to Paris and works as an architectural draughtsman until 1902.

1902

Military service with the 2e Génie (Engineer Corps) in Versailles until 1903.

1903

Refused admission to the École des Beaux-Arts, but accepted by the École des Arts Décoratifs; attends courses taught by Gabriel Ferrier and Léon Gérome at Beaux-Arts on an unofficial basis. He also enrolls at the Académie Julian. Survives with the help of André Mare, a child-hood friend, and by working as an architec-tural draughtsman and as a photographic re-toucher.

1905

Shares André Mare's studio and paints under the influence of the impressionists (*Le Jardin de ma mère*). He will destroy most of the paintings executed at this time.

1906

Spends several months in Corsica.

1907

Impressed by the Cézanne retrospective at the Salon d'Automne.

1908

Moves into La Ruche, a picturesque artists' colo-ny on the southern outskirts of Paris and lives there for three years. Meets Archipenko, Csaky, Lipchitz, Zadkine, Chagall and, possibly, Apo-llinaire and Salmon, who are already passionately interested in the new art. The other encounters described by biographers are pure invention.

1909

Paints *La Couseuse* and *Compotier sur la table*. Makes the acquaintance of Henri Rousseau and, in all probability, Robert Delaunay.

1910

Braque and Picasso's dealer D. H. Kahnweiler states that he met Léger in 1910 (but as he adds that they met after he had seen Léger's sub-mission to the Salon des Indépendants, it must have been in 1911).

1911

Makes the acquaintance of the Duchamp brothers; regular gatherings in the elder brother's studio in Puteaux, together with the Duchamps, Kupka, Delaunay, Mare, Gleizes, La Fresnaye, Le Fauconnier, Picabia, Metzinger, Ribemont-Dessaignes, Maurice Raynal and the poet Pierre Reverdy, who had recently come to Paris. Exhibits *Nus dans la forêt* at the Salon des Indépendants; Apollinaire mentions it in articles.

1912

At the Salon d'Automne, Léger exhibits *Le Passage à niveau* in the Maison Cubiste designed by Duchamp-Villon and Mare. Major exhibition with the Section d'or at Galerie La Boétie in October: Léger, the Duchamp brothers, Archi-penko, Alexandra Exter, Gleizes, Gris, Herbin, La Fresnaye, Lhote, Marcoussis, Metzinger, Picabia... Meets the poet Blaise Cendrars, who will become his great friend, at the private view.

1913

Dealer's contract with Kahnweiler. His first lecture on 'Les Origines de la peinture et sa valeur représentative', given at the Académie Wassiliev, is subsequently published in Canudo's journal *Montjoie*. Takes part in the Armory Show in New York and in Berlin's first Autumn Salon. Apollinaire publishes *Les Peintres cubistes*.

1914

Apollinaire publishes Léger's lecture 'Les Réalisation picturales actuelles' in his journal *Les Soirées de Paris*, and then five full-page reproductions of his paintings (June and July). When war is declared, Léger is mobilised as a sapper in the Engineering Corps and sent to the Argonne front, where he remains until 1916. Unable to paint, he executes many sketches.

1916

Transferred to the Verdun front as a stretcher-bearer, and is badly gassed.

1917

Hospitalized in Villepinte. Invalided out of the army at the end of the year, and is able to go back to painting. *La Partie de cartes*.

1918

Paints *Le Cirque*, *Les Acrobates*, *Les Disques*... Illustrates Cendrars's *J'ai tué*. Contract with Léonce Rosenberg's Galerie de l'Effort Moderne. Some of the drawings executed in hospital at Villepinte appear in Reverdy's journal *Nord-Sud*.

1919

One-man show at the galerie de l'Effort moderne. Illustrations for Cendars's *La Fin du monde*. *La Ville, Le Typographe*... Marries Jeanne Lohy.

1920

Meets Le Corbusier and Ozenfant, who have just launched their journal *L'Esprit moderne*. *Le Mécanicien, Le Remorqueur, Les Trois Camarades*... Illustrations for Ivan Goll's *Die Chaplinade*.

1921

Collaborates, together with Cendrars, on Abel Gance's film *La Roue*. Meets Mondrian and Van Doesburg. Frequent contact with Rolf de Maré and his associates from the Ballets suèdois: Jean Börlin, Nils Dardel, Carina Ari... *Le Grand déjeuner*. Six woodcuts for André Malraux's *Lunes en papier*.

1922

Skating Rink, a ballet based on a story-line by Canudo, opens on 20 January, with sets and costumes by Léger, music by Arthur Honegger and choreography by Börlin. Exhibits with Baumeister at the Der Sturm gallery in Berlin.

1923

Paints *Le Grand Remorqueur* and writes 'L'Esthétique de la machine'. Works with Mallet-Stevens, Cavalcanti and Autant-Lara on sets for Marcel L'Herbier's film *L'Inhumaine*. *La Création du monde*, a ballet based on a story-line by Cendrars, opens on 25 October, with sets and costumes by Léger, music by Darius Milhaud, and choreography by Börlin. Friendship with the American painter Gerald Murphy.

1924

Produces and directs the unscripted film *Le Ballet mécanique*, with the photographers Dudley Murphy and Man Ray and the composer Georges Antheil. Begins teaching at the Académie mo-derne, founded by Othon Friesz. His students include Otto Carlsund, Rik Olson, Franciska Clausen. Visits Italy (Venice, Ravenna), return-ing via Vienna. Lecture at the Sorbonne on 'Le Spectacle'. *Eléments mécaniques* and first *Compositions murales*.

1925

Exposition des Arts Décoratifs; collaborates on Mallet-Stevens's 'Ambassade' project (*Peinture murale*) and on Le Corbusier's Pavillon de l'Esprit Nouveau (*Le Balustre*). Exhibits in New York, Berlin and Moscow. Lectures at the Collège de France on 'L'Esthétique de la machine'. Ozenfant teaches at the Acadèmie Moderne. Léger begins to organize exhibitions of work by his students.

1928
Visits Berlin for the major exhibition of his work organized by the Flechtheim Gallery, and lectures on 'Actualités'. The text is published the following year by *Variétés* in Brussels.

1929
The Académie Moderne is reorganized. Léger now has Léon Gischia, Jean Marchand, Louis Marcoussis and Alexandra Exter as assistants. Advertizing and stage design become part of the curriculum.

1930
La Joconde aux clés, *Les Trois musiciens*. Visits Spain with Le Corbusier, and admires Gaudí's Sagrada Familia. Meets Alexander Calder.

1931
Léger's studio at the Académie Moderne closes. Stays with Gerald Murphy in Austria. Very impressed by his first visit to the United States. Begins a nine-year affair with Simone Herman.

1932
Publishes his impressions of America. Teaches briefly at the Grande Chaumière. Joins the Association des Ecrivains et Artistes Révolutionnaires.

1933
Visits Zurich for the Léger retrospective organized by the Kunsthaus. Travels with Le Corbusier to Greece for an architectural congress.

1934
Léger founds the Académie de l'Art Contemporain. Lecture at the Sorbonne on 'De l'Acropole à la tour Eiffel'. Exhibition of 'Objects' by Léger at Galerie Vignon. Visits Alexander Korda in London. Acting on a suggestion from Brassaï, Korda asks him to design costumes for his film *Things to Come*, adapted from the novel by H.G. Wells. Visits Stockholm, where Carlsund and R. De Maré organize an exhibition of his works. Returns to London; the project with Korda collapses.

1935
Decorates a gymnasium at the Exposition Internationale in Brussels. Visits the United States, where MOMA (New York) and the Art Institute of Chicago hold an exhibition of his works. He stays in the USA until the beginning of March 1936. Renews acquaintance with John Dos Passos, whom he had met at the Murphys' home in France. Meetings with architects.

1936
Takes an active part in the so-called 'Querelle du réalisme' debates at the Maison de la Culture. Designs sets for *David Triomphant*, a ballet by Serge Lifar with music by Vittorio Rieti (15 December). Goes on working on his *Composition aux deux perroquets* and *Adam et Eve*.

1937
A number of projects for the Exposition Internationale end in failure; he does, however, execute a panel for Mallet-Stevens's Solidarité nationale pavilion and a large mural entitled *Le Transport des forces* for the Palais de la Découverte. This was painted with the assistance of students. Lectures in Belgium and defends the Belgian painter Victor Servranckx's murals. Visits Finland for an exhibition in Helsinki, where he meets Alvar Aalto. Designs sets and costumes for *Naissance d'une cité*, a play by Jean-Richard Bloch directed by Pierre Aldebert, with music by Roger Désormière, Jean Wiener, Darius Milhaud and Arthur Honegger and choreography by Tony Grégory. Five performances are given between 18 and 22 October (and not in 1938, as Léger's biographers claim) at the Vélodrome d'Hiver. Lectures and debates in workers' clubs.

1938
Exhibition at the Palais des Beaux-Arts, Brussels. Visits the United States in September, and stays there until March 1939. Visits Dos Passos and the architect Harrison. Eight lectures at Yale University on the theme of colour in architecture. Decorates Nelson A. Rockefeller's apartment in New York.

1940
Plans decorations for a flying club near Nancy. During the 'phoney war' and the exodus, Léger is at the family farm in Lisores, and then goes to Bordeaux and Marseille. Obtains a visa for the United States, and sails for New York from Lisbon. Reaches New York in October. Lectures at Yale University, where he rejoins Darius Milhaud and other exiles.

1941
Teaches at Mills College, California, together with Milhaud. Various mural projects come to nothing. Several exhibitions in the USA. Begins the *Plongeurs* series.

1942
Exhibitions in New York. *Acrobates*.

1943
Goes to Montreal for an exhibition of his work. Meets Father Couturier. Paints landscapes: *Fleurs dans un élement mécanique*, *503*, and *L'Arbre dans l'échelle*.

1944
Collaborates with Calder, Ernst, Duchamp and Man Ray on Hans Richter's film *Dreams that Money Can Buy* ('Girl with the artificial heart' sequence). *Cyclistes* series.

1945
Several exhibitions in the United States. *La Grande Julie*. Léger joins the Parti Communiste Français. In late December, he returns to France via Le Havre and settles in Lisores.

1946
Returns to Paris in late January. Exhibits the works painted in America at the Galerie Carré. Father Couturier asks him to design a mosaic for the façade of a church in Assy (Haut Savoie); it will not be completed until 1949. *Adieu New York*. Atelier Fernand Léger reopens.

1947
From now onwards, Léger frequently exhibits throughout the world. Exhibitions in Amsterdam and Berne, with Calder.

1948
Sets and costumes for Prokofiev's ballet *Le Pas d'acier*, performed at the Théâtre des Champs Elysées in June. Visits Wroclaw in Poland for the Peace Congress. Public debate with Jean Bazaine on 'art today' in Brussels. Executes a mural with his students for the International Women's Congres at the Porte de Versailles (Paris). Illustrations for Guillevec's *Coordonnées*. Begins to paint *Loisirs*.

1949
Fifteen lithographs for Rimbaud's *Les Illuminations*. *Le Cirque*, an album of sixty lithographs. First ceramics, executed with the assistance of his former student Roland Brice. Major retrospective at the Musée d'Art Moderne, Paris. *Les Loisirs, sur fond rouge*.

1950
Death of Jeanne Léger. Major exhibition at the Tate Gallery, London. Sets and costumes for Milhaud's opera *Bolivar* at the Opéra de Paris (12 May). Maquettes for stained-glass windows for church in Audincourt. *Les Constructeurs*.

1951
Several exibitions worldwide to celebrate Léger's seventieth birthday. In Paris, there are exhibitions at the Galerie Leiris, the Galerie Maeght and the Maison de la Pensée Française, which shows *Les Constructeurs* (an illustrated booklet with texts by Claude Roy and Paul Eluard is published in connection with the exhibition). Poem-painting *Les Mains, Hommage à Mayakovsky*. Attends the Milan Triennale.

1952
Marries Nadia Khodossievitch, who has been his assistant for many years and who runs the Atelier when he is away. Moves to Le Gros-Tilleul, Gif-sur-Yvette. Monumental panel for the large auditorium of the United Nations building in New York. Visits Venice and Vienna. Exhibitions in Amsterdam, Berlin, Chicago, New York and Paris. *Femme à l'oiseau* series. Lithographs for André Frénaud's *Source entière*. *La fleur polychrome* (ceramic).

1953
Begins large-scale compositions (*Le Partie de campagne*, *La Grande Parade*); several versions will be executed. Illustrates Paul Eluard's *Liberté*. Cover and illustration for Tristan Tzara's *La face intérieure*.

1954
Definitive version of *La Grande Parade*. Stained-glass windows for the University of Caracas and church in Courfaivre (Switzerland). Maquettes for a mosaic for Gaz de France's administrative building in Alfortville, and for a mosaic for the auditorium of the Sao Paolo opera house. Major interview with Dora Vallier for *Les Cahiers d'art*: 'La Vie fait l'oeuvre de Fernand Léger'.

1955

Grand Prize, Sao Paolo Biennale. Maquette for mosaic for the Memorial Hospital, Saint-Lô (Normandy); it is in unveiled in 1956. Visits Czechoslovakia for the Spartakaides. Writes 'C'est comme ça que cela commence' as a preface to Pierre Descargues's *Fernand Léger*, which has already gone to press. This literary testament will be reprinted in the catalogue to the posthumous exhibition at the Musée des Arts Décoratifs in 1956. Drawings and lithographs for André Stil's *Levers de rideau*, which will appear shortly after his death. Retrospective at the Musée des Beaux-Arts, Lyon. Fernand Léger dies at Gif-sur-Yvette on 17 August.

In 1957, work begins on the Musée Fernand Léger in Biot; it opens on 13 May 1960.

Les Femmes aux perroquet (Women with Parrot). 1952. Ceramic relief, 33 $^1/_8$ × 48 $^3/_8$ in. (84 × 123 cm).
Musée National Fernand Léger, Biot. Gift of Nadia Léger and Georges Bauquier.

Bibliography

Writings by Fernand Léger

There is no full collected edition of Léger's many writings, which are scattered in various reviews and journals. The most important can be found in:

Fonctions de la peinture, Paris: Denoël-Gonthiers, 'collection 'Méditations', 1965; Translated as *Functions of Painting*, Ed. Edward F. Fry, with a preface by George L. K. Morris, tr. Alexandra Anderson, London: Thames and Hudson, 1973.
Mes Voyages, Paris: Editeurs Français Réunis, 1960.
Fernand Léger: Propos et prèsence (textes choisis), Paris: Seghers, 1959.

Major unpublished texts can also be found in:

Pierre Descargues, *Fernand Léger*, Paris: Cercle d'Art, 1955.
Roger Garaudy, *Pour un réalisme du XXᵉ siècle*, Paris: Grasset, 1968.
Europe no. spécial: Fernand Léger, Paris: August–September 1971.
Dora Vallier, *OL'Intérieur de l'art*, Paris: Le Seuil, 1982 (Interview with Fernand Léger).
La Querelle du réalisme, Paris: Cercle d'art, collection 'Diagonales', 1987.

References for other articles are given in the body of the text.

On Fernand Léger

As was stated earlier, the only works to have been consulted for this book are by the artist and his contemporaries: Guillaume Apollinaire, Jean Bazaine, Blaise Cendrars, Jean Epstein, Daniel H. Kahnweiler, Le Corbusier, Kasimir Malevich, Darius Milhaud, Amédée Ozenfant, Maurice Raynal, Pierre Reverdy, André Salmon, Gino Severini, Wilhelm Uhde, Maurice de Vlaminck, Christian Zervos. References are given in the body of the text.

Georges Bauquier is preparing a *catalogue raisonné* (Paris: Editions Maeght). The first volume (1903-1919) appeared in 1990; the second (1920-1924) in 1992.

Even a succinct bibliography of the literature on Fernand Léger would take up many pages. Fairly detailed bibliographies will be found in the following catalogues: *Fernand Léger*, Paris, Musée des Arts Décoratifs, 1956; C. Laugier and M. Richet, eds., *Léger*, Paris: Paris: Centre Georges Pompidou, 1981.

In addition to the works mentioned above, bibliographies recommend the following recent studies:

Christopher Glenn: *Léger and the Avant-Garde*, New Haven and London: Yale University Press, 1976.
Werner Schmalenbach, *Léger*, Paris: Cercle d'Art, 1977.
Peter de Francia, *Fernand Léger, New Haven and London: Yale University Press, 1983*.
Georges Bauquier, Léger, Paris: Maeght.
Gilles Néret, *Léger*, Paris: Casterman, 1990.

Catalogues

Léger's Le Grand Déjeuner (text by R.L. Herbert and R. Lehman), The Minneapolis Institute of Arts, 1980.
Fernand Léger 1881-1955 (G. Bauquier. D. Ruckhaberle, G. Fabre, Ch. Green), Berlin: Staatliche Kunsthalle, 1980.
Fernand Léger: la poésie de l'objet (M. Jardot, C. Derouet, M. B. Pouradier-Duteil), Paris: Musée National d'Art Moderne, 1981.
Léger et l'Esprit moderne (M. O. Briot, Cl. Fabre, B. Rose), Musée d'Art Moderne de Paris, Museum of Fine Arts, Houston, Musée Rath, Geneva, 1982.
Léger och Norden (C. Derouet, S. Gjessing, F. T. Fredriksen, O. Reuterswärd, G. Schildt), Stockholm: Moderna Museet, 1992.

ILLUSTRATIONS

1
Le Jardin de ma mère. 1905.
(My Mother's Garden)
Oil on canvas, 18 ⅛ × 15 in.
(46 × 38 cm).
Musée National Fernand Léger, Biot.
Gift of Nadia Léger and Georges
Bauquier.

2
Portrait de l'oncle de l'artiste.
1905.
(Portrait of the Artist's Uncle)
Oil on canvas, 17 ⅜ × 13 ¾ in.
(44 × 35 cm).
Musée National Fernand Léger, Biot.
Gift of Nadia Léger and Georges
Bauquier.

3

Académie d'homme. 1909.
(Male Nude)
Graphite on beige paper, 13 × 9 ⅞ in.
(33 × 25 cm).
Musée National d'Art Moderne,
Centre Georges Pompidou, Paris.

4

Nu. 1912.
(Nude)
Ink on buff paper, 11 ⅞ × 7 ⅞ in.
(30 × 20 cm).
Musée National d'Art Moderne,
Centre Georges Pompidou, Paris.

5

Le Compotier sur la table. 1909.
(Fruitbowl on Table)
Oil on canvas, 33 × 38 ⅞ in.
(83.8 × 98.7 cm).
The Minneapolis Institute of Arts,
The William Hood Dunwoody Fund.

6

6
Nus dans la forêt. 1909–1910.
(Nudes in the Forest)
Oil on canvas, 47 ¹/₄ × 67 in.
(120 × 170 cm).
Rijksmuseum Kröller-Müller
Museum, Otterlo.

7
Fumeurs. 1911.
(Smokers)
Oil on canvas, 47 ³/₄ × 38 in.
(121.4 × 96.5 cm).
Solomon R. Guggenheim Museum,
New York. Gift of Solomon R.
Guggenheim, 1938.
Photo: David Heald.

7

8

8
La Noce. 1910–1911.
(The Wedding)
Oil on canvas, 101 ¼ × 81 ⅛ in.
(257 × 206 cm).
Musée National d'Art Moderne,
Centre Georges Pompidou, Paris.

9

9
Trois Figures ou Étude pour trois portraits. 1910–1911.
(Three Figures, or Study for Three Portraits)
Oil on canvas, 76 ³/₄ × 45 ⁷/₈ in.
(195 × 116.5 cm).
Milwaukee Art Museum. Anonymous gift.

10

11

10
La Fumée. 1912.
(Smoke)
Oil on canvas, 36 ¹/₄ × 28 ³/₄ in.
(92 × 73 cm).
Albright-Knox Gallery, Buffalo, New
York. Room of Contemporary Art
Fund, 1940.

11
Modèle nu dans l'atelier.
1912–1913.
(Nude Model in the Studio)
Oil on sacking, 50 ³/₈ × 38 ¹/₈ in.
(127.8 × 95.7 cm).
Solomon R. Guggenheim Museum,
New York.
Photo: David Heald.

12
Le Passage à niveau. 1912.
(Level Crossing)
Oil on canvas, 36 ⁵/₈ × 31 ⁷/₈ in.
(93 × 81 cm).
Galerie Beyeler, Basel.
Photo: Hans Hinz.

13
La Femme en bleu. 1912.
(Woman in Blue)
Oil on canvas, 76 × 51 ¹/₄ in.
(193 × 130 cm).
Kunstmuseum, Basel.
Photo: Hans Hinz.

12

14

14
**Les Maisons dans les arbres.
Paysage n° 3**. 1914.
(Houses in the Trees. Lanscape No.3)
Oil on canvas, 51 ¹/₄ × 38 ¹/₄ in.
(130 × 97 cm).
Kunstmuseum, Basel.
Photo: Hans Hinz.

15
L'Escalier. 1913.
(Staircase)
Oil on canvas, 56 ³/₄ × 46 ¹/₂ in.
(144 × 118 cm).
Kunsthaus, Zurich.

16
L'Escalier. 1914.
(Staircase)
Oil on canvas, 56 ⁷/₈ × 36 ⁷/₈ in.
(144.5 × 93.5 cm).
Moderna Museet, Stockholm.

15

17

17
Contraste de formes. 1913.
(Contrasting Forms)
Oil on canvas, 39 $^3/_8$ × 31 $^7/_8$ in.
(100 × 81 cm).
Musée National d'Art Moderne,
Centre Georges Pompidou, Paris.
Gift of Jeanne and André Lefèvre.

18
La Cocarde, Avion brisé. 1916.
(Roundel, Wrecked Aeroplane)
Gouache, 9 $^5/_8$ × 12 in.
(24.5 × 30.5 cm).
Musée National Fernand Léger, Biot.
Gift of Nadia Léger and Georges
Bauquier.

18

19

20

21

19
Le Réveille-matin. 1914.
(Alarm Clock)
Oil on canvas, 39 $^3/_8$ × 31 $^7/_8$ in.
(100 × 81 cm).
Musée National d'Art Moderne,
Centre Georges Pompidou, Paris.
Gift of Jeanne and André Lefévre.

20
La Femme en rouge et vert. 1914.
(Woman in Red and Green)
Oil on canvas, 39 $^3/_8$ × 31 $^7/_8$ in.
(100 × 81 cm).
Musée National d'Art Moderne,
Centre Georges Pompidou, Paris.

21
Le 14 Juillet. 1914.
(The Fourteenth of July)
Oil on canvas, 28 $^3/_4$ × 23 $^5/_8$ in.
(73 × 60 cm).
Musée National Fernand Léger, Biot.
Gift of Nadia Léger and Georges
Bauquier.

22

22
Le Soldat à la pipe. 1916.
(Soldier with Pipe)
Oil on canvas, 51 ¹/₄ × 38 ¹/₄ in.
(130 × 97 cm).
Kunstammlung Nordrheim-
Westfalen, Düsseldorf.

23

23
La Partie de cartes. 1917.
(Card Game)
Oil on canvas, 50 3/8 × 76 in.
(128 × 193 cm).
Rijksmuseum Kröller-Müller, Otterlo.

24

24
Le Remorqueur rose. 1918.
(Pink Tugboat)
Oil on canvas, 26 1/4 × 36 1/4 in.
(66.5 × 92 cm).
Museum Ludwig, Cologne.
Photo: Rheinisches Bildarchiv.

25
Les Hélices. 2ᵉ état. 1918.
(Propellers. Second State)
Oil on canvas, 31 7/8 × 25 3/4 in.
(80.9 × 65.4 cm).
Collection, The Museum of Modern
Art, New York.
Gift of Katherine S. Dreier.

25

26

26
Le Cirque. 1918.
(The Circus)
Oil on canvas, 22 $^7/_8$ × 37 $^1/_4$ in.
(58 × 94.5 cm).
Musée National d'Art Moderne,
Centre Georges Pompidou, Paris.

27
Les Acrobates dans le cirque.
1918.
(Acrobats at the Circus)
Oil on canvas, 38 $^1/_4$ × 46 in.
(97 × 117 cm).
Kunstmuseum, Basel.
Photo: Hans Hinz.

27

28

28
Le Typographe. 1919.
(Typographer)
Oil on canvas, 21 1/4 × 18 1/8 in.
(54 × 46 cm).
Rijksmuseum Kröller-Müller, Otterlo.

29
La Ville. 1919.
(The City)
Oil on canvas, 93 1/8 × 120 1/4 in.
(236.5 × 305.5 cm).
Philadelphia Museum of Art:
A. E. Gallatin Collection.

29

Les Disques. 1918.
(Disks)
Oil on canvas, 94 $\frac{1}{2}$ × 74 $\frac{3}{4}$ in. (240 × 190 cm).
Musée d'Art Moderne de la Ville de Paris.

31

32

33

34

35

36

37

34
Le Pont du remorqueur. 1920.
(Deck of the Tugboat)
Oil on canvas, 38 × 51 ¼ in.
(96.5 × 130 cm).
Musée National d'Art Moderne,
Centre Georges Pompidou, Paris.
Bequest of Eva Gourgaud.

35
Le Remorqueur. 1920.
(Tugboat)
Oil on canvas, 41 × 52 in.
(104 × 132 cm).
Musée de Grenoble.
Photo: André Morin.

36
Les Disques dans la ville. 1920.
(Disks in the City)
Oil on canvas, 51 ¼ × 63 ¾ in.
(130 × 162 cm).
Musée National d'Art Moderne,
Centre Georges Pompidou, Paris.
Gift of Louise and Michel Leiris.

37
Les Trois Camarades. 1920.
(Three Comrades)
Oil on canvas, 36 ¼ × 28 ¾ in.
(92 × 73 cm).
Stedelijk Museum, Amsterdam.

38

38
L'Homme à la pipe. 1920.
(Man with Pipe)
Oil on canvas, 35 $^7/_8$ × 25 $^5/_8$ in.
(91 × 65 cm).
Musée d'Art Moderne de la Ville de
Paris. Gift of Collection Girardin.

39
La Femme au miroir. c. 1920.
(Woman with Mirror)
Oil on canvas, 36 × 25 $^3/_8$ in.
(91.5 × 64.5 cm).
Moderna Museet, Stockholm.

39

Le Mécanicien. 1920.
(The Mechanic)
Oil on canvas, 45 ⅝ × 35 in. (116 × 88.8 cm).
National Gallery of Canada, Ottawa.

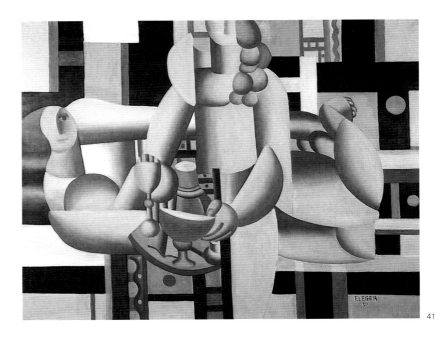

41

41
Les Deux Femmes et la nature morte. 2ᵉ état. 1920.
(Two Women and Still Life. Second State)
Oil on canvas, 28 ³/₄ × 36 ¹/₄ in.
(73 × 92 cm).
Von der Heydt-Museum, Wuppertal.

42
Nature morte au chandelier. 1922.
(Still Life with Candlestick)
Oil on canvas, 45 ⁵/₈ × 31 ¹/₂ in.
(116 × 80 cm).
Musée d'Art Moderne de la Ville de Paris.

43
Femmes dans un intérieur. 1922.
(Women in an Interior)
Oil on canvas, 25 ⁵/₈ × 36 ¹/₄ in.
(65 × 92 cm).
Musée National d'Art Moderne, Centre Georges Pompidou, Paris.

44
Le Grand Déjeuner. 1921.
(The Luncheon)
Oil on canvas, 72 ¹/₄ × 99 in.
(183.5 × 251.5 cm).
Collection, The Museum of Modern Art, New York. Mrs Simon Guggenheim Fund.

42

43

44

45

46

47

48

45
La Création du monde: Costume de Femme. 1923.
(The Creation of the World: Woman's Costume)
Watercolour, 10 $^7/_8$ × 6 $^3/_4$ in.
(27.7 × 17 cm).
Dansmuseet, Stockholm.

46
La Création du monde: Le Singe. 1923.
(The Creation of the World: Monkey)
Watercolour, 11 $^7/_8$ × 6 $^3/_4$ in.
(30 × 17 cm).
Dansmuseet, Stockholm.

47
La Création du monde: Être préhistorique. 1923.
(The Creation of the World: Prehistoric Creature)
Watercolour, 5 $^1/_2$ × 11 $^1/_4$ in.
(14 × 28.5 cm).
Dansmuseet, Stockholm.

48
La Création du monde: Coléoptère. 1923.
(The Creation of the World: Beetle)
Watercolour, 5 $^7/_8$ × 9 $^7/_8$ in.
(15 × 25 cm).
Dansmuseet, Stockholm.

49

50

49
**Projet d'affiche pour
'L'Inhumaine'**. 1923.
(Poster design for 'L'Inhumaine')
Gouache, 11 $^7/_8$ × 14 $^5/_8$ in.
(30 × 37 cm).
Private collection.

50
Skating Rink. 1922.
Watercolour, 16 × 18 $^7/_8$ in.
(40.5 × 48 cm).
Dansmuseet, Stockholm.

51

52

51
Femme tenant des fleurs. 1922.
(Woman Holding Flowers)
Oil on canvas, 28 $^{7}/_{8}$ × 45 $^{7}/_{8}$ in.
(73.3 × 116.5 cm).
Kunstammlung Nordrhein-
Westfalen, Düsseldorf.

52
La Femme et l'enfant. 1922.
(Woman and Child)
Oil on canvas, 67 $^{3}/_{8}$ × 95 in.
(171 × 241.5 cm).
Kunstmuseum, Basel.
Gift of Raoul La Roche.
Photo: Hans Hinz.

53
Paysage animé. 1924.
(Animated Landscape)
Oil on canvas, 19 $^{3}/_{4}$ × 23 $^{5}/_{8}$ in.
(50 × 60 cm).
Philadelphia Museum of Art.
Gift of Bernard Davis.

53

54

54
Le Grand Remorqueur. 1923.
(Large Tug)
Oil on canvas, 49 $\frac{1}{4}$ × 74 $\frac{3}{4}$ in.
(125 × 190 cm).
Musée National Fernard Léger, Biot.
Gift of Nadia Léger and Georges
Bauquier.

55

55
Éléments mécaniques sur fond rouge. 1924.
(Mechanical Elements on Red Background)
Oil on canvas, 36 ¹/₄ × 25 ⁵/₈ in.
(92 × 65 cm).
Musée National Fernand Léger, Biot.
Gift of Nadia Léger and Georges Bauquier.

56
La Lecture. 1924.
(Reading)
Oil on canvas, 44 ⁷/₈ × 57 ¹/₂ in.
(114 × 146 cm).
Musée National d'Art Moderne, Centre Georges Pompidou, Paris.
Bequest of Eva Gourgaud.

57
Élément mécanique. 1924.
(Mechanical Element)
Oil on canvas, 57 ¹/₂ × 38 ¹/₄ in.
(146 × 97 cm).
Musée National d'Art Moderne, Centre Goerges Pompidou, Paris.
Bequest of Eva Gourgaud.
Photo: Philippe Migeat.

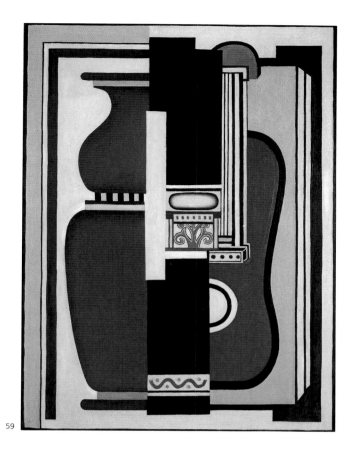

59

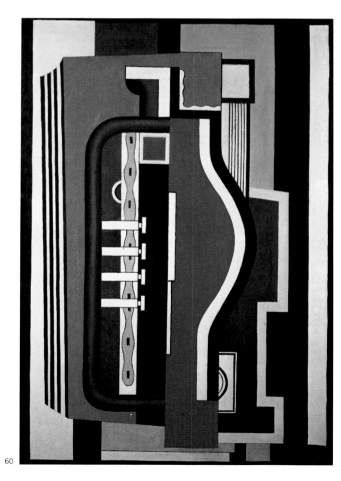

60

58
Composition murale. 1926.
(Mural Composition)
Oil on canvas, 51 ¹/₄ × 38 ¹/₄ in.
(130 × 97 cm).
Musée National Fernand Léger, Biot.
Gift of Nadia Léger and Georges
Bauquier.

59
Guitare bleue et vase. 1926.
(Blue guitar and Vase)
Oil on canvas, 51 ³/₄ × 38 ³/₈ in.
(131.5 × 97.5 cm).
Kunstmuseum, Basel.
Photo: Hans Hinz.

60
L'Accordéon. 1926.
(The Accordeon)
Oil on canvas, 51 ³/₈ × 35 in.
(130.5 × 89 cm).
Stedelijk Van Abbesmuseum,
Eindhoven.

61
Le Balustre. 1925.
(Baluster)
Oil on canvas, 51 × 38 ¼ in.
(129.5 × 97.2 cm).
Collection, The Museum of Modern Art,
New York, Mrs Simon Guggenheim Fund.

62
Roulement à billes. 1926.
(Ball-bearings)
Oil on canvas, 57 $^1/_2$ × 44 $^7/_8$ in.
(146 × 114 cm).
Kunstmuseum, Basel.
Photo: Hans Hinz.

63

64

63
Feuilles et coquillages. 1927.
(Leaves and Shells)
Oil on canvas, 51 × 38 ³/₄ in.
(129.5 × 98.5 cm).
Tate Gallery, London.
Photo: John Webb.

64
Nature morte aux feuilles vertes.
1927.
(Still Life with Green Leaves)
Oil on canvas, 36 ¹/₄ × 28 ³/₄ in.
(92 × 73 cm).
Kunstmuseum Bern, Hermann und
Margrit Ruph-Stiftung.

65

66

65
Nature morte. 1927.
(Still Life)
Oil on canvas, 44 $^7/_8$ × 57 $^7/_8$ in.
(114 × 147 cm).
Kunstmuseum Bern, Hermann und
Margrit Ruph-Stiftung.
Photo: Gerhard Howald.

66
Composition. 1929.
Oil on canvas, 23 $^5/_8$ × 36 $^1/_4$ in.
(60 × 92 cm).
Musée National d'Art Moderne,
Centre Georges Pompidou, Paris.

67

Les Trois Musiciens. 1930.
(The Three Musicians)
Oil on canvas, 46 ¹/₂ × 44 ³/₄ in.
(118 × 113.5 cm).
Von der Heydt-Museum, Wuppertal.

68
La Joconde aux clés. 1930.
(Mona Lisa with Keys)
Oil on canvas, 35 $^{7}/_{8}$ × 28 $^{3}/_{8}$ in.
(91 × 72 cm).
Musée National Fernand Léger, Biot.
Gift of Nadia Léger and Georges Bauquier.

69

70

69
La Danseuse bleue. 1930.
(Blue Dancer)
Oil on canvas, 57 $^{1}/_{2}$ × 44 $^{7}/_{8}$ in.
(146 × 114 cm).
Musée National d'Art Moderne,
Centre Georges Pompidou, Paris.

70
Nature morte (aux deux clés).
1930.
(Still Life with Two Keys)
Oil on canvas, 57 $^{1}/_{2}$ × 38 $^{1}/_{4}$ in.
(146 × 97 cm).
Musée National d'Art Moderne,
Centre Georges Pompidou, Paris.

71
Contrastes d'objects. 1930.
(Contrasting Objects)
Oil on canvas, 38 $^{1}/_{4}$ × 51 $^{1}/_{4}$ in.
(97 × 130 cm).
Musée National d'Art Moderne,
Centre Georges Pompidou, Paris.

71

72

73

74

72
La Femme à la rose. 1930.
(Woman with Rose)
Oil on canvas, 25 $^5/_8$ × 19 $^3/_4$ in.
(65 × 50 cm).
Galerie Louise Leiris, Paris.

73
La Rose. 1931.
Oil on canvas, 36 $^1/_4$ × 28 $^3/_4$ in.
(92 × 73 cm).
Galerie Louise Leiris, Paris.

74
La Danse. 1929.
Oil on canvas, 51 $^1/_4$ × 35 $^1/_2$ in.
(130 × 90 cm).
Musée de Grenoble.
Photo: André Morin.

75

76

77

75
Nature morte. 1931.
(Still Life)
Oil on canvas, 23 ⁵/₈ × 36 ¹/₄ in.
(60 × 92 cm).
Galerie Louise Leiris, Paris.

76
Paysage. 1931.
(Landscape)
Oil on canvas, 25 ⁵/₈ × 36 ¹/₄ in.
(65 × 92 cm).
Galerie Louise Leiris, Paris.

77
Composition au compas. 1932.
(Composition with Compass)
Oil on canvas, 25 ⁵/₈ × 36 ¹/₄ in.
(65 × 92 cm).
Galerie Louise Leiris, Paris.

78
Composition au parapluie. 1932.
(Composition with Umbrella)
Oil on canvas, 51 ¹/₄ × 35 in.
(130 × 89 cm).
Galerie Louise Leiris, Paris.

79
Composition aux trois figures.
1932.
(Composition with Three Figures)
Oil on canvas, 50 ³/₈ × 90 ¹/₂ in.
(128 × 230 cm).
Musée National d'Art Moderne,
Centre Georges Pompidou, Paris.

78

79

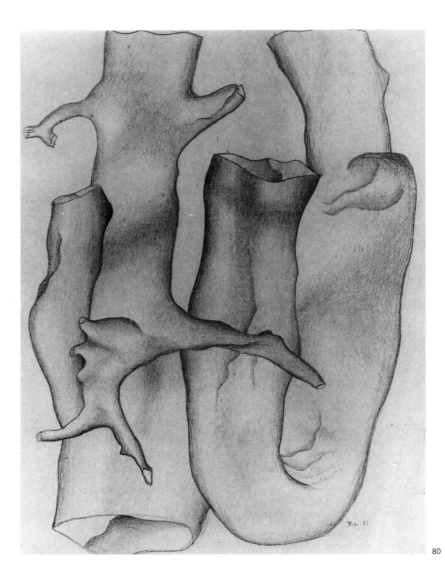

80

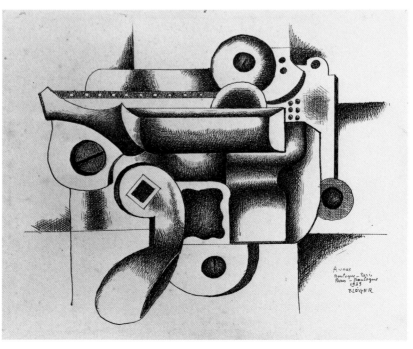

80
Arbres. 1932.
(Trees)
Coloured pencil, 25 ⅝ × 18 ⅝ in.
(65 × 48 cm).
Musée National d'Art Moderne,
Centre Georges Pompidou, Paris.

81
Serrure. 1933.
(Lock)
Ink on beige paper, 13 × 15 ⅝ in.
(33 × 39 cm).
Musée National d'Art Moderne,
Centre Georges Pompidou, Paris.

81

82

82
**Composition aux deux
perroquets**. 1935–1939.
(Composition with Two Parrots)
Oil on canvas, 157 ½ × 189 in.
(400 × 480 cm).
Musée National d'Art Moderne,
Centre Georges Pompidou, Paris.

83

La Fleur polychrome. 1936.
(Polychrome Flower)
Oil on canvas, 35 × 51 ¼ in.
(89 × 130 cm).
Galerie Louise Leiris, Paris.

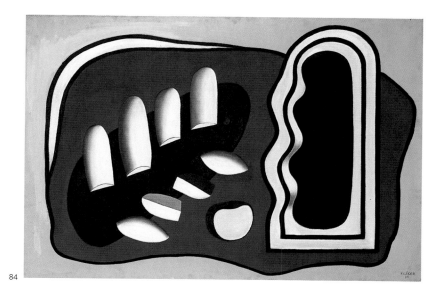

84

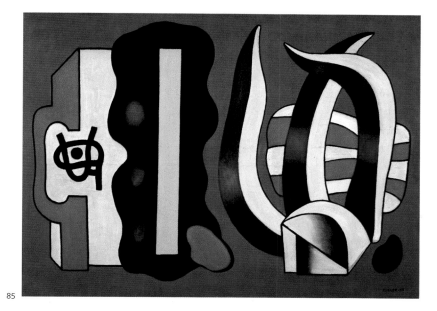

85

86

84
Composition sur fond jaune.
1936.
(Composition on Yellow Ground)
Oil on canvas, 35 × 51 1/4 in.
(89 × 130 cm).
Galerie Louise Leiris, Paris.

85
Composition à l'aloès nº 3. 1935.
(Composition with Aloe No. 3)
Oil on canvas, 38 1/4 × 51 1/4 in.
(97 × 130 cm).
Galerie Louise Leiris, Paris.

86
L'Étoile de mer. 1937.
(Starfish)
Oil on canvas, 25 5/8 × 36 1/4 in.
(65 × 92 cm).
Galerie Louise Leiris, Paris.

87
Le Transport des forces. 1937.
(The Transportation of Power)
Gouache, 24 $^3/_8$ × 39 $^3/_4$ in. (62 × 101 cm).
Musée National Fernand Léger, Biot.
Gift of Nadia Léger and Georges Bauquier.

88

89

88
Marie l'acrobate. 1934.
(Marie the Acrobat)
Oil on canvas, 28 ³/₄ × 36 ¹/₄ in.
(73 × 92 cm).
Galerie Louise Leiris, Paris.

89
Le Vase rouge et noir. 1938.
(Red and Black Vase)
Oil on canvas, 23 ⁵/₈ × 36 ¹/₄ in.
(60 × 92 cm).
Galerie Louise Leiris, Paris.

90
Composition aux trois profils.
1937.
(Composition with Three Profiles)
Oil on canvas, 35 × 51 ¼ in.
(89 × 130 cm).
Galerie Louise Leiris, Paris.

91

91
L'Arbre noir. 1937.
(Black Tree)
Oil on canvas, 36 1/4 × 25 5/8 in.
(92 × 65 cm).
Galerie Louise Leiris, Paris.

92
Le Grand coq bleu. 1937.
(Large Blue Cockerel)
Oil on canvas, 51 1/4 × 37 3/4 in.
(130 × 96 cm).
Galerie Louise Leiris, Paris.

93
Maquette pour une peinture murale. 1938.
(Maquette for Mural)
Oil on canvas, 63 3/4 × 44 7/8 in.
(162 × 114 cm).
Musée d'Art Moderne, Villeneuve-d'Asq. Gift of Geneviève and
Jean Masurel.

92

94

94

Adam et Eve. 1935–1939.
(Adam and Eve)
Oil on canvas, 89 ³/₄ × 127 ³/₄ in.
(228 × 324.5 cm).
Kunstammlung Nordrhein-
Westfalen, Düsseldorf.

95

L'Avion dans le ciel. 1939–1952.
(Aeroplane in the Sky)
Oil on canvas, 23 ⁵/₈ × 35 ¹/₂ in.
(60 × 90 cm).
Musée National Fernand Léger, Biot.
Gift of Nadia Léger and Georges
Bauquier.

96

**Projet décoratif pour un centre
d'aviation populaire**. 1940.
(Decorative Project for a Flying Club)
Graphite, watercolour and gouache,
10 ¹/₄ × 20 ⁵/₈ in.
(26 × 52.5 cm).
Musée National d'Art Moderne,
Centre Georges Pompidou, Paris.

95

96

97

98

97
Composition. 1940–1942.
Oil on canvas, 51 ¼ × 38 ¼ in.
(130 × 97 cm).
Galerie Louise Leiris, Paris.

98
L'Homme à la nature morte.
1938–1943.
(Man with Still Life)
Oil on canvas, 38 ¼ × 51 ¼ in.
(97 × 130 cm).
Galerie Louise Leiris, Paris.

99
La Racine noire. 1941.
(The Black Root)
Oil on canvas, 69 ¾ × 48 in.
(177 × 122 cm).
Galerie Maeght, Paris.

100

100
La Danse. 1942.
Oil on canvas, 72 × 60 $^5/_8$ in.
(183 × 154 cm).
Galerie Louise Leiris, Paris.

101
Les Acrobates en gris. 1942–1944.
(Acrobats in Grey)
Oil on canvas, 72 × 57 ⅝ in.
(183 × 147 cm).
Musée National d'Art Moderne,
Centre Georges Pompidou, Paris.

102

Plongeurs sur fond jaune. 1941.
(Divers on Yellow Background)
Oil on canvas, 73 ¹/₂ × 85 ³/₄ in.
(186.7 × 217.8 cm).
Art Institute of Chicago.
Gift of Mr and Mrs Maurice
E. Culberg.

103

Les Plongeurs polychromes.
1942–1946.
(Polychrome Divers)
Oil on canvas, 98 ¹/₂ × 72 ¹/₂ in.
(250 × 184 cm).
Musée National Fernand Léger, Biot.
Gift of Nadia Léger and Georges
Bauquier.

104

Les Plongeurs II. 1941–1942.
(Divers II)
Oil on canvas, 90 × 68 in.
(228.6 × 172.8 cm).
Collection, The Museum of Modern
Art, New York, Mrs Simon
Guggenheim Fund.

103

105

106

105
Le Disque rouge. 1943.
(Red Disk)
Oil on canvas, 24 × 19 ³/₄ in.
(61 × 50 cm).
Galerie Louise Leiris, Paris.

106
Composition au couteau. 1943.
(Composition with Knife)
Oil on canvas, 25 ⁵/₈ × 21 ¹/₄ in.
(65 × 54 cm).
Galerie Louise Leiris, Paris.

107
L'Arbre verte. 1944.
(Green Tree)
Oil on canvas, 20 ¹/₈ × 24 in.
(51 × 61 cm).
Galerie Louise Leiris, Paris.

108
L'Arbre dans l'échelle. 1943–1944.
(Tree in Ladder)
Oil on canvas, 71 ⁵/₈ × 49 ¹/₄ in.
(182 × 125 cm).
Galerie Louise Leiris, Paris.

107

109

109
La Grande Julie. 1945.
(Big Julie)
Oil on canvas, 44 × 50 ⁵/₈ in.
(111.8 × 127.3 cm).
Collection, The Museum of Modern
Art, New York. Acquired through
Lillie P. Bliss Bequest.

110
Adieu New York. 1946.
Oil on canvas, 51 ¼ × 63 ¾ in.
(130 × 162 cm).
Musée National d'Art Moderne,
Centre Georges Pomidou, Paris.

111

111
Le Papillon sur la roue. 1948.
(Butterfly on Wheel)
Oil on canvas, 36 $^{3}/_{8}$ × 25 $^{3}/_{4}$ in.
(92.5 × 65.5 cm).
Musée des Beaux-Arts, Lille.
Photo: Bernard.

112
Nature morte aux deux poissons.
1948.
(Still Life with Two Fish)
Oil on canvas, 25 $^{5}/_{8}$ × 36 $^{1}/_{4}$ in.
(65 × 92 cm).
Galerie Louise Leiris, Paris.

112

113

113
L'Acrobate et sa partenaire. 1948.
(Acrobat and Partner)
Oil on canvas, 51 1/4 × 63 3/4 in.
(130 × 162 cm).
Tate Gallery, London.

114

114
Les Loisirs. 1948–1949.
(Leisure)
Oil on canvas, 60 ⁵/₈ × 72 ⁷/₈ in.
(154 × 185 cm).
Musée National d'Art Moderne,
Centre Georges Pompidou, Paris.

115

115
Les Loisirs sur fond rouge. 1949.
(Leisure: Red Background)
Oil on canvas, 44 $^7/_8$ × 58 $^1/_4$ in.
(114 × 148 cm).
Musée National Fernand Léger, Biot.
Gift of Nadia Léger and Georges
Bauquier

116

117

118

116-121
Le Sacré-Coeur d'Audincourt . 1950.
(Audincourt: The Sacré-Coeur)
Six gouaches
14 ⁵/₈ × 36 ⁷/₈ in. (37 × 93.5 cm); 14 ⁵/₈ × 35 ⁷/₈ in. (37 × 91 cm);
14 ⁵/₈ × 37 in. (37 × 94 cm); 13 ³/₈ × 38 ⁷/₈ in. (34 × 98 cm);
13 ³/₈ × 38 ¹/₄ in. (34 × 97 cm); 14 ⁵/₈ × 37 in. (37 × 94 cm).
Musée National d'Art Moderne, Centre Georges Pompidou, Paris.
Photo: Jacqueline Hyde.

119

120

121

122

122
Lithograph cover for catalogue to the
Fernand Léger Retrospective, Musée
National d'Art Moderne, Paris, 1949.
8 1/2 × 6 1/4 in. (21.4 × 16 cm).

123
Black and white lithograph for
catalogue to the **Fernand Léger**
Retrospective, Musée National d'Art
Moderne, Paris, 1949. 8 1/2 × 6 1/4 in.
(21.4 × 16 cm).

124
Les Constructeurs. 1950.
(Construction Workers)
Oil on canvas, 118 1/8 × 78 3/4 in.
(300 × 200 cm).
Musée National Fernand Léger, Biot.
Gift of Nadia Léger and Georges Bauquier.

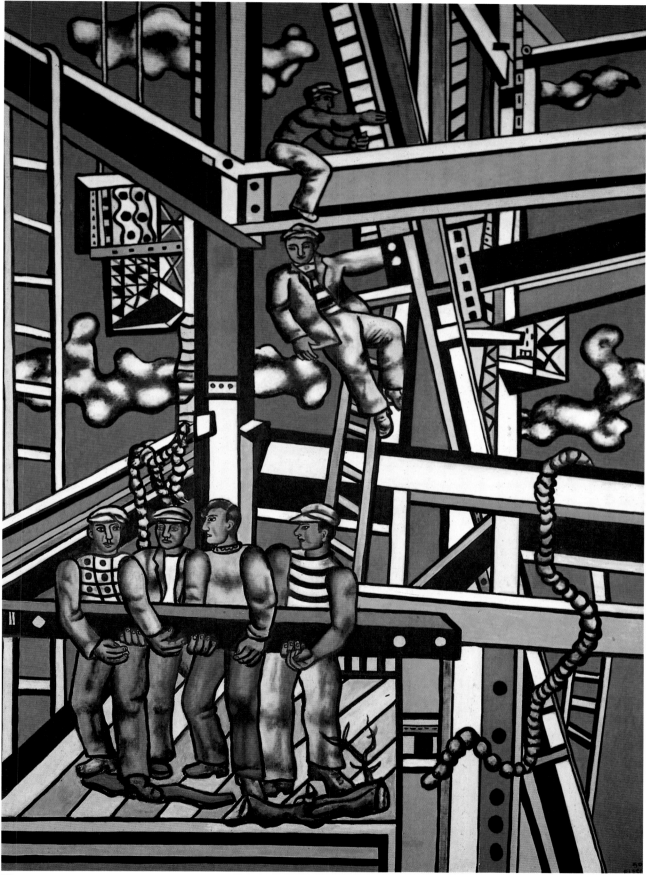

125

126

125
Les Acrobates polychromes. 1951.
(Polychrome Acrobats)
Oil on canvas, 36 ¹/₄ × 23 ⁵/₈ in.
(92 × 60 cm).
Stedelijk Van Abbesmusuem,
Eindhoven.

126
**Deux papillons jaunes sur une
échelle**. 1951.
(Two Yellow Butterflies on a Ladder)
Oil on canvas, 36 ¹/₄ × 14 ⁵/₈ in.
(92 × 37 cm).
Musée National d'Art Moderne,
Centre Georges Pompidou, Paris.
Photo: Jacqueline Hyde.

127
Les Trois Soeurs. État définitif.
1952.
(The Three Sisters. Final State)
Oil on canvas, 63 $^3/_4$ × 51 $^1/_4$ in.
(162 × 130 cm).
Staatsgalerie, Stuttgart.

128

128
Composition abstraite. 1952.
(Abstract Composition)
Ceramic relief. Height: 24 ³/₄ in.
(63 cm).
Private collection.

129
La Fleur qui marche. 1953.
(Walking Flower)
Maquette for ceramic sculpture,
26 × 20 ⁷/₈ in. (66 × 53 cm).
Musée National Fernand Léger, Biot.
Gift of Nadia Léger and Georges
Bauquier.

130
La Fleur polychrome. 1952.
Decorated plaster, 66 ¹/₂ × 53 ¹/₈ × 16 in.
(169 × 135 × 40.5 cm).
Musée National d'Art Moderne,
Centre Georges Pompidou, Paris.
Photo: Philippe Migeat.

129

131

La Grande Parade sur fond rouge. 1953.
(The Big Parade on Red Ground)
Oil on canvas, 44 $^7/_8$ × 61 in.
(114 × 155 cm).
Musée National Fernand Léger, Biot.
Gift of Nadia Léger and Georges
Bauquier.

132

Le Campeur. 1954.
(The Camper)
Oil on canvas, 118 $^1/_8$ × 96 $^1/_2$ in.
(300 × 245 cm).
Musée National Fernand Léger, Biot.
Gift of Nadia Léger and Georges
Bauquier.

La Grande Parade. État définitif. 1954.
(The Big Parade. Final State)
Oil on canvas, 117 ³/₄ × 157 ¹/₂ in.
(299 × 400 cm).
Solomon R. Guggenheim Museum,
New York.
Photo: David Heald.

134

134
La Partie de campagne. 1954.
(Outing in the Country)
Oil on canvas, 76 ¹/₂ × 76 ¹/₂ in.
(194.5 × 194.5 cm).
Museum Ludwig, Cologne,
Photo: Rheinisches Bildarchiv.

135

136

136
Le Jardin d'enfants. 1960.
(Kintergarden)
Ceramic sculpture. Height: 260 in.
(660 cm).
Musée National Fenand Léger, Biot.

137
**Relief de céramique et mosaïque
sur la façade du musée**. 1957–1960.
(Ceramic and Mosaic Relief on
Façade of Museum)
4280 sq. ft. (400 m²).
Musée National Fernand Léger, Biot.

138
**Composition aux deux oiseaux
sur fond jaune**. 1955.
(Composition with Two Birds on
Yellow Ground)
Oil on canvas, 51 ¼ × 35 in.
(130 × 89 cm).
Musée National Fernand Léger, Biot.
Gift of Nadia Léger and Georges
Bauquier.

137

List of Illustrations

22. **Le Soldat à la pipe**. 1916.
(Soldier with Pipe)
Oil on canvas, 51 $\frac{1}{4}$ × 38 $\frac{1}{4}$ in.
(130 × 97 cm).
Kunstsammlung Nordrhein-Westfalen,
Düsseldorf.

23. **La Partie de cartes**. 1917.
(Card Game)
Oil on canvas, 50 $\frac{3}{8}$ × 76 in.
(128 × 193 cm).
Rijksmuseum Kröller-Müller, Otterlo.

24. **Le Remorqueur rose**. 1918.
(Pink Tugboat)
Oil on canvas, 26 $\frac{1}{4}$ × 36 $\frac{1}{4}$ in.
(66.5 × 92 cm).
Museum Ludwig, Cologne.
Photo: Rheinisches Bildarchiv.

25. **Les Hélices**. 2e état. 1918.
(Propellers. Second State)
Oil on canvas, 31 $\frac{7}{8}$ × 25 $\frac{3}{4}$ in.
(80.9 × 65.4 cm).
Collection, The Museum of Modern Art,
New York.
Gift of Katherine S. Dreier.

26. **Le Cirque**. 1918.
(The Circus)
Oil on canvas, 22 $\frac{7}{8}$ × 37 $\frac{1}{4}$ in.
(58 × 94.5 cm).
Musée National d'Art Moderne, Centre
Georges Pompidou, Paris.

27. **Les Acrobates dans le cirque**. 1918.
(Acrobats at the Circus)
Oil on canvas, 38 $\frac{1}{4}$ × 46 in.
(97 × 117 cm).
Kunstmuseum, Basel.
Photo: Hans Hinz.

28. **Le Typographe**. 1919.
(Typographer)
Oil on canvas, 21 $\frac{1}{4}$ × 18 $\frac{1}{8}$ in.
(54 × 46 cm).
Rijksmuseum Kröller-Müller, Otterlo.

29. **La Ville**. 1919.
(The City)
Oil on canvas, 93 $\frac{1}{8}$ × 120 $\frac{1}{4}$ in.
(236.5 × 305.5 cm).
Philadelphia Museum of Art: A. E.
Gallatin Collection.

30. **Les Disques**. 1918.
(Disks)
Oil on canvas, 94 $\frac{1}{2}$ × 74 $\frac{3}{4}$ in.
(240 × 190 cm).
Musée d'Art Moderne de la Ville de Paris.

31. **Étude pour La Partie de cartes**.
1919.
(Study for Card Game)
Oil on canvas, 36 $\frac{1}{4}$ × 38 $\frac{3}{4}$ in.
(92 × 73 cm).
Staatsgalerie, Stuttgart.

32. **Contraste de formes**. 1918.
(Contrasting Forms)
Oil on canvas, 16 $\frac{1}{8}$ × 10 $\frac{1}{2}$ in.
(41 × 26.5 cm).
Musée d'Art Moderne de la Ville de Paris.

33. **Le Disque**. 1918.
(Disk)
Oil on canvas, 25 $\frac{5}{8}$ × 21 $\frac{1}{4}$ in.
(65 × 54 cm).
Collection Thyssen-Bornemisza, Lugano.

34. **Le Pont du remorqueur**. 1920.
(Deck of the Tugboat)
Oil on canvas, 38 × 51 $\frac{1}{4}$ in.
(96.5 × 130 cm).
Musée National d'Art Moderne, Centre
Georges Pompidou, Paris.
Bequest of Eva Gourgaud.

35. **Le Remorqueur**. 1920.
(Tugboat)
Oil on canvas, 41 × 52 in.
(104 × 132 cm).
Musée de Grenoble.
Photo: André Morin.

36. **Les Disques dans la ville**. 1920.
(Disks in the City)
Oil on canvas, 51 $\frac{1}{4}$ × 63 $\frac{3}{4}$ in.
(130 × 162 cm).
Musée National d'Art Moderne, Centre
Georges Pompidou, Paris.
Gift of Louise and Michel Leiris.

37. **Les Trois Camarades**. 1920.
(Three Comrades)
Oil on canvas, 36 $\frac{1}{4}$ × 28 $\frac{3}{4}$ in.
(92 × 73 cm).
Stedelijk Museum, Amsterdam.

38. **L'Homme à la pipe**. 1920.
(Man with Pipe)
Oil on canvas, 35 $\frac{7}{8}$ × 25 $\frac{5}{8}$ in.
(91 × 65 cm).
Musée d'Art Moderne de la Ville de
Paris. Gift of Collection Girardin.

39. **La Femme au miroir**. c. 1920.
(Woman with Mirror)
Oil on canvas, 36 × 25 $\frac{3}{8}$ in.
(91.5 × 64.5 cm).
Moderna Museet, Stockholm.

40. **Le Mécanicien**. 1920.
(The Mechanic)
Oil on canvas, 45 $\frac{5}{8}$ × 35 in.
(116 × 88.8 cm).
National Gallery of Canada, Ottawa.

41. **Les Deux Femmes et la nature
morte**. 2e état. 1920.
(Two Women and Still Life. Second
State)
Oil on canvas, 28 $\frac{3}{4}$ × 36 $\frac{1}{4}$ in.
(73 × 92 cm).
Von der Heydt-Museum, Wuppertal.

42. **Nature morte au chandelier**.
1922.
(Still Life with Candlestick)
Oil on canvas, 45 $\frac{5}{8}$ × 31 $\frac{1}{2}$ in.
(116 × 80 cm).
Musée d'Art Moderne de la Ville de
Paris.

43. **Femmes dans un intérieur**. 1922.
(Women in an Interior)
Oil on canvas, 25 $\frac{5}{8}$ × 36 $\frac{1}{4}$ in.
(65 × 92 cm).
Musée National d'Art Moderne, Centre
Georges Pompidou, Paris.

44. **Le Grand Déjeuner**. 1921.
(The Luncheon)
Oil on canvas, 72 $\frac{1}{4}$ × 99 in.
(183.5 × 251.5 cm).
Collection, The Museum of Modern Art,
New York. Mrs Simon Guggenheim Fund.

45. **La Création du monde: Costume
de Femme**. 1923.
(The Creation of the World: Woman's
Costume)
Watercolour, 10 $\frac{7}{8}$ × 6 $\frac{3}{4}$ in.
(27.7 × 17 cm).
Dansmuseet, Stockholm.

46. **La Création du monde: Le Singe**.
1923.
(The Creation of the World: Monkey)
Watercolour, 11 $\frac{7}{8}$ × 6 $\frac{3}{4}$ in.
(30 × 17 cm).
Dansmuseet, Stockholm.

47. **La Création du monde: Être
préhistorique**. 1923.
(The Creation of the World: Prehistoric
Creature)
Watercolour, 5 $\frac{1}{2}$ × 11 $\frac{1}{4}$ in.
(14 × 28.5 cm).
Dansmuseet, Stockholm.

48. **La Création du monde:
Coléoptère**. 1923.
(The Creation of the World: Beetle)
Watercolour, 5 $\frac{7}{8}$ × 9 $\frac{7}{8}$ in.
(15 × 25 cm).
Dansmuseet, Stockholm.

49. **Projet d'affiche pour
'L'Inhumaine'**. 1923.
(Poster design for 'L'Inhumaine')
Gouache, 11 $\frac{7}{8}$ × 14 $\frac{5}{8}$ in.
(30 × 37 cm).
Private collection.

50. **Skating Rink**. 1922.
Watercolour, 16 × 18 $\frac{7}{8}$ in.
(40.5 × 48 cm).
Dansmuseet, Stockholm.

51. **Femme tenant des fleurs**. 1922.
(Woman Holding Flowers)
Oil on canvas, 28 $\frac{7}{8}$ × 45 $\frac{7}{8}$ in.
(73.3 × 116.5 cm).
Kunstsammlung Nordrhein-Westfalen,
Düsseldorf.

52. **La Femme et l'enfant**. 1922.
(Woman and Child)
Oil on canvas, 67 $\frac{3}{8}$ × 95 in.
(171 × 241.5 cm).
Kunstmuseum, Basel.
Gift of Raoul La Roche.
Photo: Hans Hinz.

53. **Paysage animé**. 1924.
(Animated Landscape)
Oil on canvas, 19 $\frac{3}{4}$ × 23 $\frac{5}{8}$ in.
(50 × 60 cm).
Philadelphia Museum of Art.
Gift of Bernard Davis.

54. **Le Grand Remorqueur**. 1923.
(Large Tug)
Oil on canvas, 49 $\frac{1}{4}$ × 74 $\frac{3}{4}$ in.
(125 × 190 cm).
Musée National Fernard Léger, Biot.
Gift of Nadia Léger and Georges
Bauquier.

55. **Éléments mécaniques sur fond
rouge**. 1924.
(Mechanical Elements on Red
Background)
Oil on canvas, 36 $\frac{1}{4}$ × 25 $\frac{5}{8}$ in.
(92 × 65 cm).
Musée National Fernard Léger, Biot.
Gift of Nadia Léger and Georges
Bauquier.

56. **La Lecture**. 1924.
(Reading)
Oil on canvas, 44 $\frac{7}{8}$ × 57 $\frac{1}{2}$ in.
(114 × 146 cm).
Musée National d'Art Moderne, Centre
Georges Pompidou, Paris.
Bequest of Eva Gourgaud.

57. **Élément mécanique**. 1924.
(Mechanical Element)
Oil on canvas, 57 $\frac{1}{2}$ × 38 $\frac{1}{4}$ in.
(146 × 97 cm).
Musée National d'Art Moderne, Centre
Goerges Pompidou, Paris.
Bequest of Eva Gourgaud.
Photo: Philippe Migeat.

58. **Composition murale**. 1926.
(Mural Composition)
Oil on canvas, 51 $\frac{1}{4}$ × 38 $\frac{1}{4}$ in.
(130 × 97 cm).
Musée National Fernard Léger, Biot.
Gift of Nadia Léger and Georges Bauquier.

59. **Guitare bleue et vase**. 1926.
(Blue guitar and Vase)
Oil on canvas, 51 $\frac{3}{4}$ × 38 $\frac{3}{8}$ in.
(131.5 × 97.5 cm).
Kunstmuseum, Basel.
Photo: Hans Hinz.

60. **L'Accordéon**. 1926.
(The Accordeon)
Oil on canvas, 51 $\frac{3}{8}$ × 35 in.
(130.5 × 89 cm).
Stedelijk Van Abbesmuseum,
Eindhoven.

61. **Le Balustre**. 1925.
(Baluster)
Oil on canvas, 51 × 38 $\frac{1}{4}$ in.
(129.5 × 97.2 cm).
Collection, The Museum of Modern Art,
New York, Mrs Simon Guggenheim
Fund.

62. **Roulement à billes**. 1926.
(Ball-bearings)
Oil on canvas, 57 $\frac{1}{2}$ × 44 $\frac{7}{8}$ in.
(146 × 114 cm).
Kunstmuseum, Basel.
Photo: Hans Hinz.

63. **Feuilles et coquillages**. 1927.
(Leaves and Shells)
Oil on canvas, 51 × 38 $\frac{3}{4}$ in.
(129.5 × 98.5 cm).
Tate Gallery, London.
Photo: John Webb.

64. **Nature morte aux feuilles
vertes**. 1927.
(Still Life with Green Leaves)
Oil on canvas, 36 $\frac{1}{4}$ × 28 $\frac{3}{4}$ in.
(92 × 73 cm).
Kunstmuseum Bern, Hermann und
Margrit Ruph-Stiftung.

65. **Nature morte**. 1927.
(Still Life)
Oil on canvas, 44 $\frac{7}{8}$ × 57 $\frac{7}{8}$ in.
(114 × 147 cm).
Kunstmuseum Bern, Hermann und
Margrit Ruph-Stiftung.
Photo: Gerhard Howald.

66. **Composition**. 1929.
Oil on canvas, 23 $\frac{5}{8}$ × 36 $\frac{1}{4}$ in.
(60 × 92 cm).
Musée National d'Art Moderne, Centre
Georges Pompidou, Paris.

67. **Les Trois Musiciens**. 1930.
(The Three Musicians)
Oil on canvas, 46 $\frac{1}{2}$ × 44 $\frac{3}{4}$ in.
(118 × 113.5 cm).
Von der Heydt-Museum, Wuppertal.

68. **La Joconde aux clés**. 1930.
(Mona Lisa with Keys)
Oil on canvas, 35 $\frac{7}{8}$ × 28 $\frac{3}{8}$ in.
(91 × 72 cm).
Musée National Fernand Léger, Biot.
Gift of Nadia Léger and Georges
Bauquier.

69. **La Danseuse bleue**. 1930.
(Blue Dancer)
Oil on canvas, 57 $\frac{1}{2}$ × 44 $\frac{7}{8}$ in.
(146 × 114 cm).
Musée National d'Art Moderne, Centre
Georges Pompidou, Paris.

70. **Nature morte (aux deux clés)**.
1930.
(Still Life with Two Keys)
Oil on canvas, 57 $\frac{1}{2}$ × 38 $\frac{1}{4}$ in.
(146 × 97 cm).
Musée National d'Art Moderne, Centre
Georges Pompidou, Paris.

71. **Contrastes d'objects**. 1930.
(Contrasting Objects)
Oil on canvas, 38 $\frac{1}{4}$ × 51 $\frac{1}{4}$ in.
(97 × 130 cm).
Musée National d'Art Moderne, Centre
Georges Pompidou, Paris.

72. **La Femme à la rose**. 1930.
(Woman with Rose)
Oil on canvas, 25 $\frac{5}{8}$ × 19 $\frac{3}{4}$ in.
(65 × 50 cm).
Galerie Louise Leiris, Paris.

73. **La Rose**. 1931.
Oil on canvas, 36 $\frac{1}{4}$ × 28 $\frac{3}{4}$ in.
(92 × 73 cm).
Galerie Louise Leiris, Paris.

74. **La Danse**. 1929.
Oil on canvas, 51 $\frac{1}{4}$ × 35 $\frac{1}{2}$ in.
(130 × 90 cm).
Musée de Grenoble.
Photo: André Morin.

75. **Nature morte**. 1931.
(Still Life)
Oil on canvas, 23 $\frac{5}{8}$ × 36 $\frac{1}{4}$ in.
(60 × 92 cm).
Galerie Louise Leiris, Paris.

76. **Paysage**. 1931.
(Landscape)
Oil on canvas, 25 $\frac{5}{8}$ × 36 $\frac{1}{4}$ in.
(65 × 92 cm).
Galerie Louise Leiris, Paris.

77. **Composition au compas**. 1932.
(Composition with Compass)
Oil on canvas, 25 $\frac{5}{8}$ × 36 $\frac{1}{4}$ in.
(65 × 92 cm).
Galerie Louise Leiris, Paris.

78. **Composition au parapluie**. 1932.
(Composition with Umbrella)
Oil on canvas, 51 $\frac{1}{4}$ × 35 in.
(130 × 89 cm).
Galerie Louise Leiris, Paris.

79. **Composition aux trois figures**. 1932.
(Composition with Three Figures)
Oil on canvas, 50 $^3/_8$ × 90 $^1/_2$ in.
(128 × 230 cm).
Musée National d'Art Moderne, Centre
Georges Pompidou, Paris.

80. **Arbres**. 1932.
(Trees)
Coloured pencil, 25 $^5/_8$ × 18 $^5/_8$ in.
(65 × 48 cm).
Musée National d'Art Moderne, Centre
Georges Pompidou, Paris.

81. **Serrure**. 1933.
(Lock)
Ink on beige paper, 13 × 15 $^5/_8$ in.
(33 × 39 cm).
Musée National d'Art Moderne, Centre
Georges Pompidou, Paris.

82. **Composition aux deux perroquets**. 1935-1939.
(Composition with Two Parrots)
Oil on canvas, 157 $^1/_2$ × 189 in.
(400 × 480 cm).
Musée National d'Art Moderne, Centre
Georges Pompidou, Paris.

83. **La Fleur polychrome**. 1936.
(Polychrome Flower)
Oil on canvas, 35 × 51 $^1/_4$ in.
(89 × 130 cm).
Galerie Louise Leiris, Paris.

84. **Composition sur fond jaune**. 1936.
(Composition on Yellow Ground)
Oil on canvas, 35 × 51 $^1/_4$ in.
(89 × 130 cm).
Galerie Louise Leiris, Paris.

85. **Composition à l'aloès n° 3**. 1935.
(Composition with Aloe No. 3)
Oil on canvas, 38 $^1/_4$ × 51 $^1/_4$ in.
(97 × 130 cm).
Galerie Louise Leiris, Paris.

86. **L'Étoile de mer**. 1937.
(Starfish)
Oil on canvas, 25 $^5/_8$ × 36 $^1/_4$ in.
(65 × 92 cm).
Galerie Louise Leiris, Paris.

87. **Le Transport des forces**. 1937.
(The Transportation of Power)
Gouache, 24 $^3/_8$ × 39 $^3/_4$ in.
(62 × 101 cm).
Musée National Fernand Léger, Biot.
Gift of Nadia Léger and Georges Bauquier.

88. **Marie l'acrobate**. 1934.
(Marie the Acrobat)
Oil on canvas, 28 $^3/_4$ × 36 $^1/_4$ in.
(73 × 92 cm).
Galerie Louise Leiris, Paris.

89. **Le Vase rouge et noir**. 1938.
(Red and Black Vase)
Oil on canvas, 23 $^5/_8$ × 36 $^1/_4$ in.
(60 × 92 cm).
Galerie Louise Leiris, Paris.

90. **Composition aux trois profils**. 1937.
(Composition with Three Profiles)
Oil on canvas, 35 × 51 $^1/_4$ in.
(89 × 130 cm).
Galerie Louise Leiris, Paris.

91. **L'Arbre noir**. 1937.
(Black Tree)
Oil on canvas, 36 $^1/_4$ × 25 $^5/_8$ in.
(92 × 65 cm).
Galerie Louise Leiris, Paris.

92. **Le Grand coq bleu**. 1937.
(Large Blue Cockerel)
Oil on canvas, 51 $^1/_4$ × 37 $^3/_4$ in.
(130 × 96 cm).
Galerie Louise Leiris, Paris.

93. **Maquette pour une peinture murale**. 1938.
(Maquette for Mural)
Oil on canvas, 63 $^3/_4$ × 44 $^7/_8$ in.
(162 × 114 cm).
Musée d'Art Moderne, Villeneuve-d'Asq.
Gift of Geneviève and Jean Masurel.

94. **Adam et Eve**. 1935-1939.
(Adam and Eve)
Oil on canvas, 89 $^3/_4$ × 127 $^3/_4$ in.
(228 × 324.5 cm).
Kunstammlung Nordrhein-Westfalen,
Düsseldorf.

95. **L'Avion dans le ciel**. 1939–1952.
(Aeroplane in the Sky)
Oil on canvas, 23 $^5/_8$ × 35 $^1/_2$ in.
(60 × 90 cm).
Musée National Fernand Léger, Biot.
Gift of Nadia Léger and Georges
Bauquier.

96. **Projet décoratif pour un centre d'aviation populaire**. 1940.
(Decorative Project for a Flying Club)
Graphite, watercolour and gouache,
10 $^1/_4$ × 20 $^5/_8$ in. (26 × 52.5 cm).
Musée National d'Art Moderne, Centre
Georges Pompidou, Paris.

97. **Composition**. 1940–1942.
Oil on canvas, 51 $^1/_4$ × 38 $^1/_4$ in.
(130 × 97 cm).
Galerie Louise Leiris, Paris.

98. **L'Homme à la nature morte**. 1938–1943.
(Man with Still Life)
Oil on canvas, 38 $^1/_4$ × 51 $^1/_4$ in.
(97 × 130 cm).
Galerie Louise Leiris, Paris.

99. **La Racine noire**. 1941.
(The Black Root)
Oil on canvas, 69 $^3/_4$ × 48 in.
(177 × 122 cm).
Galerie Maeght, Paris.

100. **La Danse**. 1942.
Oil on canvas, 72 × 60 $^5/_8$ in.
(183 × 154 cm).
Galerie Louise Leiris, Paris.

101. **Les Acrobates en gris**. 1942–1944.
(Acrobats in Grey)
Oil on canvas, 72 × 57 $^5/_8$ in.
(183 × 147 cm).
Musée National d'Art Moderne, Centre
Georges Pompidou, Paris.

102. **Plongeurs sur fond jaune**. 1941.
(Divers on Yellow Background)
Oil on canvas, 73 $^1/_2$ × 85 $^3/_4$ in.
(186.7 × 217.8 cm).
Art Institute of Chicago. Gift of Mr and
Mrs Maurice E. Culberg.

103. **Les Plongeurs polychromes**. 1942–1946.
(Polychrome Divers)
Oil on canvas, 98 $^1/_2$ × 72 $^1/_2$ in.
(250 × 184 cm).
Musée National Fernand Léger, Biot.
Gift of Nadia Léger and Georges
Bauquier.

104. **Les Plongeurs II**. 1941–1942.
(Divers II)
Oil on canvas, 90 × 68 in.
(228.6 × 172.8 cm).
Collection, The Museum of Modern Art,
New York. Mrs Simon Guggenheim Fund.

105. **Le Disque rouge**. 1943.
(Red Disk)
Oil on canvas, 24 × 19 $^3/_4$ in.
(61 × 50 cm).
Galerie Louise Leiris, Paris.

106. **Composition au couteau**. 1943.
(Composition with Knife)
Oil on canvas, 25 $^5/_8$ × 21 $^1/_4$ in.
(65 × 54 cm).
Galerie Louise Leiris, Paris.

107. **L'Arbre verte**. 1944.
(Green Tree)
Oil on canvas, 20 $^1/_8$ × 24 in.
(51 × 61 cm).
Galerie Louise Leiris, Paris.

108. **L'Arbre dans l'échelle**. 1943–1944.
(Tree in Ladder)
Oil on canvas, 71 $^5/_8$ × 49 $^1/_4$ in.
(182 × 125 cm).
Galerie Louise Leiris, Paris.

109. **La Grande Julie**. 1945.
(Big Julie)
Oil on canvas, 44 × 50 $^5/_8$ in.
(111.8 × 127.3 cm).
Collection, The Museum of Modern Art,
New York. Acquired through Lillie P.
Bliss Bequest.

110. **Adieu New York**. 1946.
Oil on canvas, 51 $^1/_4$ × 63 $^3/_4$ in.
(130 × 162 cm).
Musée National d'Art Moderne, Centre
Georges Pomidou, Paris.

111. **Le Papillon sur la roue**. 1948.
(Butterfly on Wheel)
Oil on canvas, 36 $^3/_8$ × 25 $^3/_4$ in.
(92.5 × 65.5 cm).
Musée des Beaux-Arts, Lille.
Photo: Bernard.

112. **Nature morte aux deux poissons**. 1948.
(Still Life with Two Fish)
Oil on canvas, 25 $^5/_8$ × 36 $^1/_4$ in.
(65 × 92 cm).
Galerie Louise Leiris, Paris.

113. **L'Acrobate et sa partenaire**. 1948.
(Acrobat and Partner)
Oil on canvas, 51 $^1/_4$ × 63 $^3/_4$ in.
(130 × 162 cm).
Tate Gallery, London.

114. **Les Loisirs**. 1948–1949.
(Leisure)
Oil on canvas, 60 $^5/_8$ × 72 $^7/_8$ in.
(154 × 185 cm).
Musée National d'Art Moderne, Centre
Georges Pompidou, Paris.

115. **Les Loisirs sur fond rouge**. 1949.
(Leisure: Red Background)
Oil on canvas, 44 $^7/_8$ × 58 $^1/_4$ in.
(114 × 148 cm).
Musée National Fernand Léger, Biot.
Gift of Nadia Léger and Georges
Bauquier

116-121. **Le Sacré-Coeur d'Audincourt**. 1950.
(Audincourt: The Sacré-Coeur)
Six gouaches
14 $^5/_8$ × 36 $^7/_8$ in. (37 × 93.5 cm);
14 $^5/_8$ × 35 $^7/_8$ in. (37 × 91 cm);
14 $^5/_8$ × 37 in. (37 × 94 cm);
13 $^3/_8$ × 38 $^7/_8$ in. (34 × 98 cm);
13 $^3/_8$ × 38 $^1/_4$ in. (34 × 97 cm);
14 $^5/_8$ × 37 in. (37 × 94 cm).
Musée National d'Art Moderne, Centre
Georges Pompidou, Paris.
Photo: Jacqueline Hyde.

122. Lithograph cover for catalogue to
the **Fernand Léger** Retrospective,
Musée National d'Art Moderne, Paris,
1949. 8 $^1/_2$ × 6 $^1/_4$ in. (21.4 × 16 cm).

123. Black and white lithograph for
catalogue to the **Fernand Léger**
Retrospective, Musée National d'Art
Moderne, Paris, 1949. 8 $^1/_2$ × 6 $^1/_4$ in.
(21.4 × 16 cm).

124. **Les Constructeurs**. 1950.
(Construction Workers)
Oil on canvas, 118 $^1/_8$ × 78 $^3/_4$ in.
(300 × 200 cm).
Musée National Fernand Léger, Biot.
Gift of Nadia Léger and Georges
Bauquier.

125. **Les Acrobates polychromes**. 1951.
(Polychrome Acrobats)
Oil on canvas, 36 $^1/_4$ × 23 $^5/_8$ in.
(92 × 60 cm).
Stedelijk Van Abbesmusuem,
Eindhoven.

126. **Deux papillons jaunes sur une échelle**. 1951.
(Two Yellow Butterflies on a Ladder)
Oil on canvas, 36 $^1/_4$ × 14 $^5/_8$ in.
(92 × 37 cm).
Musée National d'Art Moderne, Centre
Georges Pompidou, Paris.
Photo: Jacqueline Hyde.

127. **Les Trois Soeurs**. État définitif. 1952.
(The Three Sisters. Final State)
Oil on canvas, 63 $^3/_4$ × 51 $^1/_4$ in.
(162 × 130 cm).
Staatsgalerie, Stuttgart.

128. **Composition abstraite**. 1952.
(Abstract Composition)
Ceramic relief. Height: 24 $^3/_4$ in. (63 cm).
Private collection.

129. **La Fleur qui marche**. 1953.
(Walking Flower)
Maquette for ceramic sculpture,
26 × 20 $^7/_8$ in. (66 × 53 cm).
Musée National Fernand Léger, Biot.
Gift of Nadia Léger and Georges Bauquier.

130. **La Fleur polychrome**. 1952.
(Polychrome Flower)
Decorated plaster, 66 $^1/_2$ × 53 $^1/_8$ × 16 in.
(169 × 135 × 40.5 cm).
Musée National d'Art Moderne, Centre
Georges Pompidou, Paris.
Photo: Philippe Migeat.

131. **La Grande Parade sur fond rouge**. 1953.
(The Big Parade on Red Ground)
Oil on canvas, 44 $^7/_8$ × 61 in.
(114 × 155 cm).
Musée National Fernand Léger, Biot.
Gift of Nadia Léger and Georges
Bauquier.

132. **Le Campeur**. 1954.
(The Camper)
Oil on canvas, 118 $^1/_8$ × 96 $^1/_2$ in.
(300 × 245 cm).
Musée National Fernand Léger, Biot.
Gift of Nadia Léger and Georges
Bauqier.

133. **La Grande Parade**. État définitif. 1954.
(The Big Parade. Final State)
Oil on canvas, 117 $^3/_4$ × 157 $^1/_2$ in.
(299 × 400 cm).
Solomon R. Guggenheim Museum,
New York.
Photo: David Heald.

134. **La Partie de campagne**. 1954.
(Outing in the Country)
Oil on canvas, 76 $^1/_2$ × 76 $^1/_2$ in.
(194.5 × 194.5 cm).
Museum Ludwig, Cologne,
Photo: Rheinisches Bildarchiv.

135. **La Partie de campagne**. 1954.
(Outing in the Country)
Oil on canvas, 96 $^1/_2$ × 118 $^1/_2$ in.
(245 × 301 cm).
Fondation Maeght, Saint-Paul.
Gift of M. and A. Maeght, 1964.
Photo: Claude Germain.

136. **Le Jardin d'enfants**. 1960.
(Kintergarden)
Ceramic sculpture. Height: 260 in.
(660 cm).
Musée National Fenand Léger, Biot.

137. **Relief de céramique et mosaïque sur la façade du musée**. 1957–1960.
(Ceramic and Mosaic Relief on Façade of
Museum)
4280 sq. ft. (400 m²).
Musée National Fernand Léger, Biot.

138. **Composition aux deux oiseaux sur fond jaune**. 1955.
(Composition with Two Birds on Yellow
Ground)
Oil on canvas, 51 $^1/_4$ × 35 in.
(130 × 89 cm).
Musée National Fernand Léger, Biot.
Gift of Nadia Léger and Georges Bauquier.